Chronic Kids, Constant Hope

Other Crossway books by Elizabeth M. Hoekstra

Keeping Your Family Close When Frequent Travel Pulls You Apart
Just for Moms
Just for Girls

All Creation Sings
A Season of Stillness
A Season of Gladness
A Season of Rejoicing
A Season of Grace

CHRONIC
KIDS
CONSTANT
HOPE

*Help and Encouragement
for Parents of Children with
Chronic Conditions*

Elizabeth Hoekstra
& Mary Bradford

CROSSWAY BOOKS • WHEATON, ILLINOIS
A DIVISION OF GOOD NEWS PUBLISHERS

Cover design: Liita Forsyth

Cover photos: The Stock Market
        Photographers: Ariel Skelly, Charles Auguste, Ronnie Kaufman

First printing 2000

Printed in the United States of America

Scripture taken from the *Holy Bible: New International Version®*. Copyright © 1973, 1978, 1984 by International Bible Society. Used by permission of Zondervan Publishing House. All rights reserved.

The "NIV" and "New International Version" trademarks are registered in the United States Patent and Trademark Office by International Bible Society. Use of either trademark requires the permission of International Bible Society.

Scripture marked KJV is taken from the King James Version of the Bible.

Library of Congress Cataloging-in-Publication Data
Hoekstra, Elizabeth, 1962-
  Chronic kids, constant hope : help and encouragement for parents of children with chronic conditions / Elizabeth Hoekstra, Mary Bradford.
    p.   cm.
  Includes bibliographical references.
  ISBN 1-58134-184-9 (pbk. : alk. paper)
  1. Parents of chronically ill children—Religious life. 2. Chronic diseases in children—Religious aspects—Christianity. I. Bradford, Mary, 1960- II. Title
BV4596.P33 H64   2000
248.8'45—dc21   00-009201
                                             CIP

15	14	13	12	11	10	09	08	07	06	05	04	03	02	01	00
15	14	13	12	11	10	9	8	7	6	5	4	3	2	1	

DEDICATED TO OUR SONS
Jordan Peter Sterling Hoekstra and Robert Thomas Bradford
Who meet each day with infectious smiles and dignity

CONTENTS

	Acknowledgments	9
	Introduction	11
1	Everyone Has a Story, What's Yours?	15
2	The Year of Firsts	27
3	When You're Mad at God	41
4	Praying for Healing	55
5	Releasing Guilt and Blame	67
6	The Family Unit	77
7	Brothers and Sisters	91
8	Educating Yourself	105
9	When Friends Say Hurtful Things . . . and They Will	121
10	"Mommy, Why?" and Other Hard Questions	133
11	Away from Home	145
12	Educational Choices	155
13	Taking Care of You	167
14	Expecting Joy	181
	Appendix	191
	Helpful Scripture Verses	203
	Notes	205

ACKNOWLEDGMENTS

Many people deserve recognition and thanks for enabling us to bring into print our experiences, our insights, and our heart-felt prayers.

Our Lord and heavenly Father has entrusted us each with a child who requires extra love, time, and nurture. We feel humbled that He would choose us for this honorable parenting role. All glory belongs to Him.

To our families, particularly our husbands, Peter and Dana, we owe gratitude for patience and understanding as we took time away from the family to work diligently on this book. A special thank you to our children for their maturity at the times when we heard them say quietly to one another, "Sshhh, Mom's working." We appreciate our daughters in particular, Holly Bradford and Geneva Hoekstra, for being our "little women" in taking over some household responsibilities. Also we owe them thanks for writing and sharing their feelings about being older siblings to chronic children.

A resounding thanks to our faithful agent Leslie Stobbe for his heart to teach and encourage, as well as for representing us and this book with conviction.

To our parents, Thomas and Cynthia Marriner, who equipped us to become the best parents we could be. A heart-felt thanks especially to our mom, who wept as a grandmother over our children's stories but marked the manuscript as a seasoned editor.

Our sincerest gratitude to our editor, Lila Bishop, for her light touch and to all the Christ-honoring, committed people at Crossway Books. Our thanks to Good News Publishers for faithfully bringing Christ into people's homes and lives.

Our thanks to the composite families whose stories and comments we used to bring experience beyond our own to the subject. We are grateful for the added depth this has given the book. And we especially thank Dr. Fay Migotsky for her encouragement and insights.

We are indebted to our sons' doctors for literally taking our children's lives into their hands. Mary would like to thank Dr. Sol Rockenmacher and Dr. Keane, pediatric cardiologists, and Dr. Mayer, pediatric cardiovascular surgeon, for being Robbie's lifelong advocates. Elizabeth is grateful for the Boston Joslin Diabetes Center, and particularly for Dr. Lori Laffel and Nurse Kristen Rice, who provide Jordan with exemplary care.

And, of course, we are thankful for our boys. Though at times a bit dubious, they showed a willingness to be vulnerable that inspired us repeatedly. We are profoundly grateful to see the Lord forging their characters into His likeness.

INTRODUCTION

When Mary's son Robbie was still an infant, someone blithely said to her (even before she was a writer), "Someday you'll write a book about this."

Then nine years later, when Elizabeth's son was diagnosed with a chronic disease at the age of six, a friend said to her, "I bet you'll write about this someday."

Little did those friends know how prophetic their words were.

Initially, however, we felt offended. What did people see in both of us that made them think we would *want* to write about mothering and raising our chronic children? It seemed a very private, lonely role; why would we want to advertise our pain?

But over the course of several years the Lord showed us that nothing is circumstantial, particularly in Christian families with chronic children. We realized that it wasn't coincidence that both of us as sisters would have chronic children. Was there a larger plan at work? Were our friends right? Should we tell our stories and offer people the much-needed hope we lacked in the first few months and years after our sons were diagnosed? Had we been equipped to hold out a mantle of practical wisdom and encouragement through God's Word to minister to others?

We believe we have. To echo Mordecai's words to a frightened Esther, "And who knows but that you have come to royal position for such a time as this?" Through our own hurt, disappointment, and grief, which the Lord has turned into His favor, we've been prepared for this "such a time" to reach out to you, our reader.

This book is not meant as a diagnostic or medical guide of any sort. We do not address specific diseases, illnesses, or conditions. Though we both hold nursing degrees, we offer the enclosed insights only as parents to other parents. We encourage you to read it slowly. In the appendix we've provided the addresses and web sites of a number of organizations that may help you better understand your child's condition. We've also included a topical Scripture index so you can search for God's help at times of particular need.

By our estimation, at least one-third of families in the United States are raising a child with a chronic condition. Chronic means that the condition is not imminently life-threatening, but rather is life-altering for the entire family. The condition may fall anywhere on the spectrum from mild asthma to a severe handicap that puts one in a wheelchair. These children who live with chronic conditions are nothing short of heroes. On their journey to courage and nobility they learn how to overcome obstacles, find creative ways to adjust, and they often develop an uncanny maturity beyond their years. But their rise to spiritual and personal confidence depends on you, their parents. We too have felt the weight of that responsibility.

We have recognized three crucial areas, as addressed throughout *Chronic Kids*, that affect your child's long-term well-being:

1) The empowering act of encouraging your child to see his or her worth in Christ, thereby developing wholeness in spirit.

2) The hope we *always* find in God's plan and Word.

3) The necessary task of building an unshakable family unit.

Whatever the chronic condition may be, your role as parents is to communicate God's infinite love for these children *as they are*, to help build a positive self-image and vision *for who they can become*, and to nurture a strong family bond that will surround and support them *whenever they need it*.

In no way do we want to appear to be taking advantage of, or profiting from, our children's lives. Our sons are young men of God with extreme compassion and sensitivity for people. They both have expressed a desire to help others. To that end, we each have decided to donate a portion of the proceeds from this book to mission work or to charities in our sons' names.

Over the months we've been preparing this book, our thoughts have been on you, our readers, your families, and especially your children. Our prayer parallels Paul's in 2 Thessalonians 1:11-12:

We constantly pray for you, that our God may count you worthy of his calling, and that by his power he may fulfill every good purpose of yours and every act prompted by your faith. We pray this so that the name of our Lord Jesus may be glorified in you, and you in him, according to the grace of our God and the Lord Jesus Christ.

1

MARY

I'm trying to bring some order into my chaotic thoughts. It's amazing how quickly my life has changed since as a newborn, Robbie was diagnosed with a congenital heart condition, and our future has taken on a completely different look. Already memories have taken on the quality of "remember when," and future plans seem to be abandoned. I feel as though I'm living in a holding pattern—disembodied—like an airplane circling an airport waiting for the controller to tell my family and me it's okay to land, disembark, and pick up the pieces of our lives to begin again.

EVERYONE HAS A STORY— WHAT'S YOURS?

The Lord is my strength and my song; he has become
my salvation. He is my God, and I will praise him,
my father's God, and I will exalt him.

EXODUS 15:2

MARY'S STORY

"It's a boy!"

The doctor held up our squalling son for my husband and me to get our first look. Dana squeezed my hand. "His name will be Robert Thomas, after his grandfather." He kissed me lightly on the forehead.

A few hours later, our pediatrician nervously fingered his stethoscope as he told us that Robbie had a very loud, persistent heart murmur. I wasn't unduly alarmed. As a nurse I knew that many babies are born with murmurs that spontaneously resolve themselves over a few days.

He coughed discreetly. "I think this is more than a patent ductus. I'd like to send you to see a heart specialist."

We brought Robbie home and watched him struggle to breathe, eat, and even stay awake. I knew something was terribly wrong.

Four days later we met with a pediatric cardiologist at a large teaching hospital in central New Hampshire. While performing an echocardiogram to diagnose the problem, the physician quickly determined that Robbie's condition was critical and deteriorating rapidly. The clinical diagnosis was truncus arterioses with coarctation of the aorta. Whoa! Even as a nurse I felt overwhelmed! How could such a tiny creature possibly have something so big and scary wrong with his heart?

Robbie was rushed to the Pediatric Intensive Care Unit to be stabilized before being transferred to Boston Children's Hospital. We had to leave him in the hospital to go home, pick up our two-year-old daughter, pack some clothes, and meet the ambulance in Boston. As we turned to leave the ICU, I shook the cardiologist's hand to say good-bye and thank you. He shocked me with his words: "Oh, you'll be seeing me again. We'll be following Robbie closely for the rest of his life." It wasn't until that moment that I realized we were only at the beginning of a long and difficult road.

They let us into the ICU to say good-bye to Robbie, and a nurse handed me his baby blanket. My husband was in a hurry to leave, as we had an hour and a half drive home before traveling two hours farther south to Boston. He copied the directions to where we were going and spun on his heel to catch the elevator. Dana was so intent on getting home that he didn't realize I was still standing in the middle of the hall shaking my head and twisting the yellow baby blanket around and around my wrist.

"Honey?"

"I can't," I whispered. "I can't just leave him here. Don't ask that of me."

"Sweetheart, we don't have a choice. He's in the best hands possible. There isn't anything more you can do for him here, but you can be there to greet him when he arrives in Boston, okay?" He gently put his arm around my shoulders and coaxed me out of the hospital.

Robbie arrived in the pediatric ICU at Children's Hospital in Boston on Christmas Eve. On Christmas Day surgeons performed a cardiac catheterization to enable them to make a plan for surgery. I sat in the waiting room outside the cath lab and watched the local news, thinking, "Why isn't this being announced as a news story? Doesn't the world realize my life has been turned upside down and inside out?"

At seven days old Robbie went through seven hours of surgery to repair his heart defect. There are no words to describe that time of waiting during his surgery. I felt numb and panicky at the same time. This couldn't possibly be happening to me! I wanted to cry to God: "This is TOO MUCH! You are asking more of me than what I can possibly do!" I asked my mother to pray that if Robbie was going to die, God would take him during surgery. I didn't see how I could possibly bring him home after surgery only to have him die later.

It is now twelve years since Robbie was born. In some respects life is easier; we have a routine established; we deal with doctors and such when we have to, and the rest of the time we carry on like a normal family. There are times though when the emotions are as raw and fresh as on the day we left Robbie in the ICU. Holidays, anniversaries, and even seeing a healthy newborn boy can trigger unexpected responses in me.

Robbie's heart defect has required further surgery, multiple cardiac catheterizations, and frequent doctors' visits. And there are many more to come. His speech development was delayed, and he has problems with coordination and gross and fine motor skills. He's had extensive speech therapy and occupational therapy. But through it all we are delighted when he makes progress, and we stubbornly refuse to set limits on what he can accomplish.

We all have a story—a personal tale that has shaped our being. This story encompasses our past and our present. It tells of our culture, family traditions, circumstances, and personal decisions. Our ongoing story equips us for the future. Through reflection on our past we can approach the unfolding of the Lord's plan with more knowledge and confidence.

Your child's story, particularly of his or her chronic condition, is a continuum of your story. Of course, your child's story is not limited to just the child. There are many characters in that story: your family, your community, your church family, your child's teachers, and medical professionals. All the elements weave together to create a complex, multifaceted, colorful tale for others to hear and thus be encouraged. It can seem like a huge responsibility though. The Lord has given you this story of your chronic child whose condition can be frustrating, scary, and overwhelming. Have you given much thought to your story and your child's? Has the Lord shown you how this story about your child can be used for His glory?

We'd like to ask you to tell your child's story. We know this can be painful. We know it can cause you to relive emotions you've successfully navigated before. But part of our prayer for this book is that it will help you, your family, and your child embrace his or her story as a crucial piece of your family's history that can be used to glorify God.

When your child's story started, you didn't know the end. Maybe that was the hardest part. Of course, you wanted assurances that the story would be guaranteed a happy resolution.

But with chronic children there is no resolution—that's what makes them chronic! We may desire resolution, but chronic means permanent (unless the Lord chooses to heal your child—more on that later). Chronic doesn't mean terminal or temporary. Though we may not understand it, in this permanence the Lord can best be glorified.

Think back to the beginning, to the time when you knew a story had begun to take root, the time when you knew your life had just changed—dramatically, forcefully, and eternally. At the beginning of the story came uncertainty and fear. All of our stories include the initial emotions: the wounded, panic-raising, blinding, choking, "NO! Not my child!" There's no way to mute the intensity of confusion and anger at what seems to be a betrayal. So it was with Elizabeth's story . . .

ELIZABETH'S STORY

The doctor said pointedly, "It's what you think it is."

"Can I have a nervous breakdown now?" I choked, trying to make the moment lighter.

"You're entitled," he said. Then shaking his head and turning away, he added more softly, "You're entitled."

As any life-altering moment stays etched forever in a person's memory, I know the time was 9:35 A.M. on October 12, 1997, a cool but bright day. All the panic I had guarded in my heart for weeks rose in my throat. This couldn't be happening!

The pediatrician pointed me to the telephone. I cuddled six-year-old Jordan in my lap and picked up the phone to call my husband, Peter, who was waiting at home with our daughter to hear the news. I couldn't see the pad of numbers on the phone, I couldn't remember my number, my hands wouldn't stop shaking. When Peter picked up after the first ring, I couldn't talk. I breathed out one word, "Diabetes."

He said, "I'll be right there."

I've always said that an overwhelming desire to protect a child is the mark of a mother's love. And that coupled with denial had kept me from seeking the doctor's diagnosis earlier. All the signs of diabetes were there: thirst, weight loss, pallor, wetting the bed, fatigue, dehydration, crankiness, but I attributed them all to Jordan's just entering first grade. I had rationalized it all away: "It's a big change for a six-year-old to be gone from home all day. Of course he'll be tired. Naturally he's thirsty if he's not getting enough to drink at school. He's a little stressed about the changes, so he's wetting the bed—no big deal."

Two things finally ripped a hole in my denial. When I cleaned around the base of the toilet, I found a buildup of sticky residue (Jordan has never had good aim), indicating a huge amount of sugar in his urine. Then two days later he started vomiting and hallucinating. I knew I couldn't hold off the inevitable any longer.

My greatest fear about taking him to the doctor, beyond the definitive diagnosis, was that the doctor would hand me a bottle of insulin, say, "You're a nurse—figure it out," and send me home. As a nurse I should have known better! But as a mother first, all my nursing knowledge left my brain. This was my child. I rationalized that if I didn't get him diagnosed, our lives wouldn't change, and he wouldn't have this life-threatening disease.

Jordan was transferred by ambulance from our local community hospital to a larger hospital with a juvenile diabetes program. I learned a few days later that his blood sugar at the time of his diagnosis was 1250 (normal is 70-110). I knew enough to realize I had literally pushed Jordan's life to the limit. Without insulin and treatment he would have died within twelve to twenty-four hours.

Then began the arduous task of learning about blood sugar control: administering shots to a scared, reluctant, squirmy little boy; balancing his food requirements with insulin and exercise; limiting his stress levels. This became all our family thought about and talked about. It consumed every one of my waking and sleeping moments.

When Jordan came home from the hospital, he had serious issues about his identity. He felt "on display" everywhere we went. Indicating anyone around us, he would frequently ask, "Do they know?" He looked like any other energetic, healthy six-year-old, but he was sure that the word diabetes hung over him like a cloud.

We resolved to help him embrace his disease, learn how to care well for himself, and grow into a godly man with sure hope for the future. That doesn't mean we didn't cry or ask the Lord why. But it does mean that Peter and I did and still do know that the Lord has entrusted us with this child with a chronic condition because we are the best people to prepare him for his life. We can only consider it an honor and a privilege to raise Jordan.

We have found encouragement in Psalm 144:12, which offers a promise to all parents: "Then our sons in their youth will be like well-nurtured plants, and our daughters will be like pillars carved to adorn a palace." Don't you find great hope and comfort in those words?

THREE REASONS WHY WE NEED A "STORY"

Have you ever seen someone at the beach or in the store or at the market, and you just *know* there is an interesting story to their lives? Maybe it's the clothes they're wearing, or maybe it's the array of international children at their feet, or maybe they walk with a limp. Propriety stops us from asking, "Excuse me, but what's your story?" (It takes a child to ask sometimes!) Of course you never know how such a query will be met either. Some find despair, pain, and hopelessness in their story and don't feel free to share their life-changing experience. But some enjoy telling their story, particularly if it encourages another person or offers hope.

That's where we come in with our children. What better way to testify to the Lord's faithfulness, provision, and protection than to share our stories with others? Proverbs 10:21 says, "The lips of the righteous nourish many." Wouldn't you like your story to "nourish many?"

Offering Timely Words

> *A man finds joy in giving an apt reply—and how good is a timely word! (Proverbs 15:23)*

An apt reply—a solid but concise answer to the inevitable questions.

ELIZABETH

Once while vacationing in Florida, we needed to give Jordan insulin while out for dinner at a restaurant. Usually Peter draws up the insulin and gives Jordan the shot in the privacy of the men's room. For some reason this time Peter drew up the insulin at the dinner table. The waiter saw what we were doing and asked which of us had diabetes. My initial rabid-mother response was to snap, "None of your business!" But as quickly as that reply came to mind, it was replaced with a more gentle answer. I smiled at Jordan and said, "Our son does."

The waiter then just about pulled up a chair as he embarked on a lengthy conversation with us about his cousin with diabetes, telling us how active this young man was. We shared with him a bit of Jordan's story and how we knew God's hand was on Jordan. The waiter went on to advise us about various places of interest nearby, gave us a coupon for a ride at Busch Gardens, and thereafter gave us great service!

This was a "timely word" on both counts. Our waiter encouraged us with his story about his active diabetic cousin, and I believe we encouraged him with our words of trust in the Lord.

Being Imitators
Be imitators of God, therefore, as dearly loved children.
(Ephesians 5:1)

The second reason you need your child's story ready on your lips is for his sense of identity. Your child needs to be confident of his importance to God. He must possess such a strong confidence that he is made in the image of Christ that nothing can make him doubt his place in God's family.

He can even be an image-bearer in talking about his disease. How he conducts himself is a representation not only of who he is, but of who God is. He needs to be taught that his disease is part of his identity, but not all of it. Your child's ability to understand and communicate about his disease ultimately equips him with confidence—confidence in his abilities, assurance of his place in life, and conviction that his chronic condition cannot separate him from who he is in Christ.

MARY

Through all of Robbie's procedures and evaluations, the professionals with whom he has come in contact have all had a similar comment. They are amazed and impressed with Robbie's high self-esteem and confidence in his worth. I think part of the explanation is that Robbie's condition is the way his life has always been; he doesn't know anything different. But I think even more important were our consistent prayers and verbal encouragement for Robbie to grow into Christlikeness. So when he's been extra kind to his sister or offers up a prayer for others, we affirm him and tell him that this is pleasing to the Lord.

Wonderfully Made
For you created my inmost being; you knit me together in my mother's womb. I praise you because I am fearfully and wonderfully made. (Psalm 139:13-14)

The third reason for having a story is to relay God's perfect plan. He knit *every* person together; each person is designed "fearfully," intricately, and wonderfully. Disease is a direct result of the Fall, and ever since, human beings have been subject to various illnesses. If God does not heal your child's condition, then He is allowing it for a purpose, and the Lord Almighty does not make mistakes.

Sometimes it's tempting to think that the Lord was absent while your child was forming in utero. We might wonder if God was temporarily looking the other direction. The question comes to our lips: "Where were You when my child was being 'knit together'?" But He was there, tenderly and gently forming your child. It wasn't a grand scheme of manipulation; it was an intentional direction of combining components to create in your child a unique individual.

CLAIMING A PROMISE

Men swear by someone greater than themselves, and the oath confirms what is said and puts an end to all argument. Because God wanted to make the unchanging nature of his purpose very clear to the heirs of what was promised, he confirmed it with an oath. God did this so that, by two unchangeable things in which it is impossible for God to lie, we who have fled to take hold of the hope offered to us may be greatly encouraged. We have this hope as an anchor for the soul, firm and secure. It enters the inner sanctuary behind the curtain, where Jesus, who went before us, has entered on our behalf. (Hebrews 6:16-20)

We love the imagery of the anchor of hope—hope that comes from God's unchanging plan and purpose and foretold promises. We can certainly grab hold of that well-embedded anchor! What a comfort to know that God has distinct promises for each individual. The promises may take on added meaning as the years go by or as other promises are added. Do you have a scriptural promise for your child? Is there a verse that offered you comfort or encouragement when you were pregnant, possibly even before you knew that your child would be different?

James 1:17 was such a verse for Elizabeth, offering assurance and a sense of the permanence of God's divine plan.

ELIZABETH

> *A month before Jordan was born, I asked the Lord for a verse for him. I had done the same thing before my daughter Geneva was born, and at that time I had found a verse that spoke of the Lord's jewels. The verse I felt the Lord showed me for Jordan was James 1:17: "Every good and perfect gift is from above, coming down from the Father of the heavenly lights, who does not change like shifting shadows."*
>
> *I hadn't looked at that verse in earnest until a few weeks after Jordan was diagnosed with diabetes. The promise of God's sovereignty and His unalterable plans encouraged me. Just because Jordan's diagnosis was new to me didn't mean it was new to the Lord. God was going to use this effect of the Fall in His comprehensive plan for Jordan. Nothing had changed in God's purpose for Jordan's life; only my perception had changed.*

The Bible offers so much hope and assurance. All we need to do is look. We encourage you to find a promise for your child and for her future. Then memorize it with your child and the rest of the family. Take Jeremiah 29:11 to task, for example: "'For I know the plans I have for you,' declares the Lord, 'plans to prosper you and not to harm you, plans to give you hope and a future.'"

In the coming chapters we will follow the theme of relaying your child's story as an avenue to minister and witness to others through the hope that is always found in the Lord. We'll help you develop your children's confidence and esteem as they learn of their value derived from God's perfect design for their lives and bodies. We'll assist you and your family in staying united as we talk about communication, taking time for yourselves, and making decisions. But most important, we want you to know you are not alone in raising your chronic kid. We've been where you are right now, and we've likely experienced the same emotions that you struggle with.

One of our father's favorite hymns is "Blessed Assurance." Hearing his bass voice sing this when we were children embedded the words in our hearts and ultimately prepared us for living the refrain: "This is my story, this is my song, praising my Savior all the day long; This is my story, this is my song, praising my Savior all the day long." Each child's story, when it focuses on God's love and faithfulness, is a story of praise to the Lord, worthy of song. Won't you sing with us a song of praise for your unique child?

PRACTICAL MATTERS

Consider writing out your child's story. Add it to a scrapbook or design a new scrapbook, journal, or photo album for your child. Add milestones to this document in the coming years as a gift to give to your child when he or she is older. Write in it your verse of hope. Even consider setting the verse to an existing tune or make up your own music.

2

When my daughter was first diagnosed with severe asthma and allergies, I couldn't take in all the doctor told us. We'd have to buy all sorts of new equipment to clean the house, special covers for her bed, and machines and medicines to help her breathe more easily. We'd have to carry a shot of epinephrine with us in case she went into anaphylactic shock again.

It was overwhelming. How were we going to pay for this? How would we make all the necessary changes? How would I personally be affected? I didn't want to deal with it.

My wife and I took turns in the hospital as our daughter stabilized, but all I wanted to do was go back to work. At least I knew how to do that. At least I could try to make more money to cover all the added expenses. My feelings of inadequacy with all the medical stuff completely shredded my confidence.

Cliff—father of nine-year-old Melanie

THE YEAR OF FIRSTS

There is a time for everything, and a season for every activity
under heaven . . . a time to weep and a time to laugh,
a time to mourn and a time to dance.

ECCLESIASTES 3:1, 4

Our parents, who were raised in the greater Boston area, have rem-
nants of a Massachusetts accent (you know, "Pahk yah cah in Havahd
Yaad"). Consequently they have always pronounced "trauma",
"trama," as if one has been hit by a tram. In some way they are right.
Our personal traumas left both of us feeling as if we'd been hit by a
tram.

When a blow to your child's health hits you, you feel run over,
flattened, and breathless. Once the crisis phase has passed, you pick
yourself up, dust off debris, scrub away the skid marks left by the
tram, and get on with life.

Then immediately you are faced with a bunch of "first times."
After the initial diagnosis, whether this happened shortly after your
child was born or later, you find yourself staggering through The Year
of Firsts.

The first time you go out in public.

The first trip to church.

The first walk through the grocery store.

The first time you leave your child with a sitter or relative.

The first birthday celebration.

The first explanation to outsiders.

The first Easter, Thanksgiving, and Christmas.

The first vacation.

The first virus or sickness.

The first time you fill out a form that requires you to write in your child's diagnosis.

The first anniversary of your child's diagnosis.

Each one brings a haunting reminder of the permanence of your child's condition. It doesn't take vacations. It doesn't close down for the holidays. It isn't hidden from view. If anything, your child's condition feels more pronounced during The Year of Firsts.

This year is like an introduction to the rest of your child's life. Similar to an introduction in a book, the first year is an overview of what you can expect ahead. The first year prepares you for future decisions as you gather information. Similarly, this chapter in this book is an overview of what you'll face in the coming years.

MARY

The first time I took Robbie to the grocery store, I had him bundled in the front pack to protect him as much as possible from the weather and from people breathing on him. At the checkout counter a grandmother-type exclaimed over my daughter Holly's curls and then reached for the front pack to get a glimpse at the tiny bundle inside. Nervously I shielded Robbie's face.

"Oh, such a tiny baby," she cooed. "And so precious! Is it a boy or a girl?" She didn't even wait for an answer but went right on, "What does it matter as long as it's healthy, right?" She patted Holly's cheek and moved away before I had even let out my pent-up breath.

I wasn't ready for the stab that went through my heart when she glibly assumed he was healthy. I put my groceries on the conveyer belt with trembling hands, shaken by the encounter. I wondered how she would have responded if I had said, "Well, he isn't healthy. He went through hours of open-heart surgery, he has a huge scar, and he can't even eat properly." It made me realize I needed to have a story to tell!

The first year after diagnosis forces us to constantly reevaluate, be prepared, and have the story on our lips. Each first pulls at our hearts because it's all a new experience. Each first is a hurtful scratch at the barely healed initial shock and pain. Old ways of doing things are gone. Old traditions and habits have to be revised or reevaluated.

Each situation or circumstance in the past was approached with a certain routine or knowledge of how you would generally do things—for vacations you'd pack clothes, belongings, etc. Now you need to add medications, emergency numbers, perhaps even research what hospitals and doctors are available at your destination. For past holidays your family gathered for traditional fare and fun, but now you have to revamp the entire meal plan for a child with special food needs. All these preparations become routine as the Year of Firsts fades into years two and three, but the first time is likely to include serious planning and much second-guessing.

There's an element of dread with firsts too—uncertainty about how it's going to work out or anxiety about how you'll cope. You question, "Am I correctly prepared? Have I thought of everything? Do I have explanations ready? Do I have plans A, B, and C in mind?" An awful lot of time goes into being ready to face the unknowns!

"I remember the *first* time . . ." is often how you reflect on your child's condition too. You'll find that as time passes, you begin to use those firsts as a guide for being prepared for other firsts. And the dread, anxiety, and fear lessen until you suddenly find yourself at the anniversary date, ready to step into year two—more equipped and in a better position emotionally and spiritually to handle it. Be encouraged by this: Once you've gone through the first time for anything, you don't have to do it again. That's the value of the "firsts"—*they aren't repeated!*

A STRANGER IN A STRANGE LAND

During the Year of Firsts you find yourself in a place where you never thought you'd be. You suddenly are kin to a group of people or families with the same condition. And you don't necessarily want to "belong" to their group. You carry the title of your child's diagnosis on a heavy heart. You may feel that you suddenly are in relationship with a fraternity that you didn't want to join, are unprepared to be connected with, and yet can't be excused from either.

You are indeed a stranger in a strange land without the benefit of a detailed map or compass. You can't see where the refreshing water is, you don't know where the dangerous cliffs are, you haven't found where shelter is, and you can't be sure of recognizing quicksand. You know there are bound to be trouble spots for you, your child, and your family in the coming months, and you want to be as prepared as possible. But looking out across the seemingly sparse landscape of your lives after a new diagnosis, it's a scary, lonely scene.

Fortunately, you do have a Guide. The One who can help you navigate this time of confusion and direction-seeking is the same One who helped the Israelites navigate their first year through the wilderness. Were they scared? Yes! Were they uncertain of the future? Yes! Were they confused about the route the Lord was leading them on? Yes! Did they grumble when provisions weren't immediately obvious? Yes!

Over and over the Lord tested them for the next *forty years*! But what was the purpose of the whole wilderness experience? To teach them to trust that God would provide, protect, remain present, and guide their steps into His future plans.

What is the divine truth of our wilderness times during The Year of Firsts? GOD IS FAITHFUL. Right after the Lord defeated the Egyptians by drowning them in the Red Sea, the Israelites sang a song of praise to the Lord: "Who among the gods is like you, O Lord? Who is like you—majestic in holiness, awesome in glory, working wonders? . . . In your unfailing love you *will lead* the people you have redeemed. In your strength you *will guide* them to your holy dwelling" (Exodus 15:11, 13, italics ours). Is this the same God who is in charge of your child and your family? You bet! From the Israelites we can borrow this overcomers' song of praise to the Lord and the promise of His direction.

FEELING OUT OF CONTROL

It's so hard to relinquish the tight control we think we have on our children's lives! Yes, the Lord has entrusted our children to us to raise to the best of our ability. But *control* them? We're only fooling ourselves if we think we have full power over everything in their lives. That's what makes raising a chronic child so difficult. In a number of diseases *control* is the key word for optimal health. Diabetes, asthma, cystic fibrosis, allergies, digestive and food absorption diseases, epilepsy, and many others require tight management of various elements. We're even told by the doctors that our children's long-term health is dependent on our control of the disease now.

What we're talking about here is really two different types of control though. One is physical, and the other is spiritual.

Medical Control

The medical approach of maintaining a balance between elements gives us a sense of staying between the parameters of control that physicians have set out for us. Medications restore missing and vital factors to your child's body. Certain foods ensure a properly functioning digestive system. Minimizing environmental hazards can help to maintain the ability to breathe. This control offers us some hope of protection from future complications.

This is what we would call "good control"—good because it is something you can do and should do to prevent future problems. Also teaching your child control over the factors that influence his or her chronic condition will help to prepare your child for a life independent of you. A friend of ours who has a child with severe Attention Deficit Disorder with hyperactivity puts it this way: "I am constantly reminding my children that my most important job is to prepare them to live without me."

Spiritual Control

The other type of control is an attempt to wrestle your child's future from the safe grip of God's hands. Of course we want guarantees that our medical control will eliminate all future problems for our children. It can't. God may allow your child to struggle through this disease for many years. Or His plan may allow your child to die before adulthood. Or perhaps your child will never live independently. Or maybe your child will develop long-term, painful complications and require constant care. Or God may choose to heal your child. We can't know the "end" of your child's chronic condition, but we can know it is already all mapped out by the Lord. He's got it covered.

We certainly have a responsibility to follow medical advice, pray for direction, and make biblical decisions, but ultimately God is God, and He's in charge of the outcome. Charles Swindoll in *Intimacy with the Almighty* says it this way: "Nothing under His control can ever be out of His control."[1]

I was still grieving daily, even hourly, three months after my son David was born with Down Syndrome. At the age of forty my worst fears of having a challenging child had come true. I was in an emotional and spiritual wasteland, completely out of control, and unable to see God anywhere in my circumstances.

At work one day I griped and moaned about how hard it was to have a child with Down Syndrome. A coworker turned to me and said quietly, "At least your son will never hurt you the way mine has hurt me." She had recently discovered her son was using drugs.

I realized that there are no guarantees with any child. I knew from birth on that I would have troubles with David, yet here was someone experiencing deep pain from a son who was "normal." Perhaps she was right—my child would probably never be involved in that kind of trouble. I then gave thanks for my precious son and felt a sense of peace rise within me. My spiritual wrestling lessened from that point on, and I was able to relinquish my desire for control back over to the Lord.

Faith—mother of six-year-old David

HOW YOU COPE

People respond to stress in different ways. Some have refined coping skills; others can't seem to get a handle on how to cope at all. It's not as if we walk through our lives intentionally preparing for a crisis either. It's a learn-as-you-go process. Each person involved in a crisis must pull in every ounce of skill, draw on every scriptural promise, and develop new ways of coping to be able to push through the first year.

In Chinese the word *crisis* is interpreted as danger plus opportunity. Your response to the "danger" of the crisis of a chronic condition presents you with an "opportunity" to develop new and effective ways of coping. You'll find yourself coping and responding on three different levels during the Year of Firsts—emotionally, spiritually, and physically.

Responding Emotionally

Emotionally, your brain interprets the crisis as a danger to your well-being. You may feel as though you want to come close, gather in, form a tight huddle. You may shut out the rest of the world and focus on this one crisis. Or, conversely, you may find yourself chattering nervously about your crisis to anyone with ears. Either way, your brain begins to automatically weed out the extraneous, unimportant things so that all your emotional energy can be committed to the life-altering event.

Responding Physically

When catastrophe (physical or emotional) strikes, adrenaline is released in your body. This acts as a buffer between you and the pain, giving a "fight or flight" response. You stand up, square your shoulders, roll up your sleeves, and fight back, or you shrink back, turn on your heel, and take flight. What's important to recognize during The Year of Firsts is that even if your tendency is to take flight, you will develop the ability to absorb the blows of information. It may take some time, but as you grow accustomed to your child's chronic condition, you'll find that the flight-inducing fear dissipates bit by bit as you gain knowledge and understanding of the disease or condition.

Responding Spiritually

We've dedicated the entire next chapter to your spiritual response to your child's condition. It's important to remember in the loneliness of the initial diagnosis that God ordains all of our steps, and He uses everything in our lives to bring us into closer fellowship with Him. Romans 5:3-5 reminds us: "Suffering produces perseverance; perseverance, character; and character, hope. And hope does not disappoint us, because God has poured out his love into our hearts by the Holy Spirit, whom he has given us." Isn't it comforting to know that our hope in the Lord *will not be disappointed!*

CONNECTING WITH OTHERS

It seems there are basically two types of people in this world when it comes to personal pain, suffering, or loss: Those who have grappled with fire and trial and those who haven't . . . yet. It's inevitable that people will experience pain in their lives at some point.

Because of the relational nature that the Lord created in us, we need to and desire to connect with others. The problem is that not everyone is able to "hear" your story or understand your pain. Even people in your family don't cope and respond the same way you do.

We are surrounded by hurting people. A mutual friend's husband died at the age of thirty-two of colon cancer. Another friend has lost her only two sons in their early twenties. Elizabeth has a friend who lives with chronic pain. Why are these people a big part of our lives? We gravitate to them because we share the common bond of pain, loss, and suffering. With these people we don't have to keep a stiff upper lip or pretend we "have it all together." We can cry, rant, and bare our inner fears, knowing these emotions are "safe" in the hands of pain-carrying friends. Simply put, we can be *real*. During the Year of Firsts these kinds of friends are truly life-savers.

But what about the rest of the population? The have-not-yet-experienced-pain-or-loss people? What about when they give hollow encouragement or ask questions while simultaneously glancing around looking for an escape route? During The Year of Firsts it's hard enough to assimilate what you're feeling, how you're going to cope, take in all the new medical and technical information, and keep your family functioning—never mind how to respond to other people's questions! This is when it's so important to have a story ready to relay. It gives you an out. When you repeat it often enough, it gives you an objective way to relate without falling apart or "dumping" all your pain on someone else.

EMOTIONAL TRIGGERS

During this first year your emotions are frequently barely hidden behind your eyes or covered by your skin. Slight, even imperceptible, events can trigger a release of emotions that may surprise even you. A trigger may be in the form of a memory, an event, a smell, a look from your child, certain clothes, insensitive words from someone, a particular place, etc. For Elizabeth a trigger is a steep hill near the hospital where Jordan was diagnosed. She remembers sitting in the back of the ambulance with Jordan and stopping at the bottom of that hill. Now every time she drives down that hill, the memory of the tense fear washes over her.

Church tends to be a trigger point for many families. There you're surrounded by people who care about you and ask questions. You're open to the Lord ministering to you during worship times. Church can be a safe place to express your grief, or, conversely, the grief can feel overwhelmingly fresh and unbearable.

Other people may find family gatherings a trigger. They feel that their child is on display and being compared to the other children. Even seeing any healthy child can cause feelings of sadness. Mary finds that seeing a healthy newborn baby boy can send a wave of grief over her—even twelve years later.

It's important to know that these triggers can happen anytime, anyplace. A trigger may catch you off guard—try to be prepared. Having your story ready to talk about, tissues ever present in your pocket, and a personal memory verse of promise will all help to lessen the potential overwhelming impact of a trigger event.

PHOTOGRAPHIC MEMORIES

Another trigger is photographs of your child. They have the ability to affect you in a deep way, and yet they are integral to your child's positive self-image and to your family's health.

ELIZABETH

Jordan had his school pictures scheduled to be taken two days after arriving home from the hospital. He wouldn't be rejoining his classroom for several more days, but in our attempt to return to "normal" life, I agreed to bring him to school at the appointed time for his individual and class photos. He acted horribly. I felt utterly embarrassed and helpless as he fought and screamed and cried about having his picture taken. Finally, after much manipulation and promises of a trip to Wal-Mart, he complied. When I got the school pictures back, I immediately regretted my forcefulness in having them taken. In the picture he was so pale, so thin, so obviously ill that it broke my heart. It was a guilt-producing and painful visual reminder of what diabetes had done to him.

I displayed it for a year on my bedroom dresser until I switched it to the following year's school pictures. I couldn't avoid placing it in the frame next to his sister's new picture, and I couldn't keep the previous year's picture. What would that have said to Jordan? That he wasn't acceptable at the time of his diagnosis? That how he looked was offensive to me, and I had to hide it?

Over the course of the year I actually came to cherish the photo, mostly because of his improvement. I could use that picture as a yardstick to measure how well he was growing, regaining weight and getting color back on his cheeks. Now that picture vividly reminds me of Jordan at that time in his life— and I'm grateful to have it permanently recorded.

I look at any picture of him now, and immediately my mind dates it as either pre-diagnosis or post-diagnosis. If it's pre-

diagnosis, I'll peer at the face in the picture and look for any sign
of the insidious disease lurking behind his eyes or in his body. I
know it's there, and I can't help but feel a sense of betrayal that
I, his mother who knows so much about him, didn't foresee or
anticipate this one hugely critical piece of his life.

Thinking again about the Israelites fleeing Egypt—what did God do to remind them of His presence and power? He provided a pillar of fire by night and a cloud by day as a visual reminder of His continual presence. He knew that what they could see with their eyes they would more readily believe.

Our children need to have a visual reminder of God's awesome power working in their lives too. Providing a photographic account of times when they were first diagnosed, or in the hospital, or sick, can show them the presence of God in the midst of their lives. You can say to your child, "Remember when this was taken? You were having blood drawn. You kept reciting the verse, 'When I am afraid I will trust in You.' I was so proud of you that day!" Or, "I love this picture of you before you had your operation. I know how brave you were trying to be. God gave you courage and protected you. Isn't He wonderful?"

Later you can use these photos as a jumping-off point to initiate conversations about his story. "How did you feel when you were in the hospital? I was worried about you." But be realistic too. Your child may cry, not want to talk about his feelings, or even revert to younger behavior. Remember, not everything in a story has to be happy, and it's important for your child to feel free to express feelings.

Taking photos of everyday events and milestones such as birthdays, a visit to the zoo, a trip to the ocean, and so on, will also increase his self-esteem. It relays that you value everything that is happening in his life and your life as a family. If we take pictures only of the "happy" times, are we sending a message of discomfort or lack of acceptance of the difficult times? Happy and difficult photos act as a visual reminder of our love and acceptance of *all* the parts of their lives.

Photographs can also be valuable as a teaching tool for people who don't understand the rigors of raising a chronic kid. In sharing your child's photo album, by leaving it on the coffee table or showing it to guests, you communicate that you're still a regular family. "See? Here we are in the hospital waiting for surgery. Robbie had all the nurses in stitches when he put on those huge pink-framed glasses. We can get pretty silly even in the midst of difficult days." Photos with stories help to break down the barriers so often erected between friends when one is dealing with a crisis.

The Year of Firsts is a roller-coaster ride. Some days you're at the top, looking across your life and feeling a moment of connection with the world—a feeling that everything will be okay. But then something happens—maybe a virus hits, or you have a difficult visit to the doctor, or you read something worrisome about your child's condition, or a friend inadvertently says something hurtful, and your roller-coaster car suddenly careens down a slope and takes your breath away all over again.

Expect these highs and lows. They're normal. The grieving process—which we'll cover in the next chapter—doesn't fall into a neat little checklist with each step getting crossed off as you move on to the next step.

The highs and lows of The Year of Firsts, however, ultimately prepare you for the years ahead. Your coping mechanisms are challenged, and you develop a more confident way of dealing with stress. Your communication skills are stretched, and you learn how to talk through needs, issues, and expectations. Through this you, your child, and your family are growing stronger as individuals and closer as a family.

PRACTICAL MATTERS

Experts warn us that periods of great stress are not the best time to make major decisions. Mary's family considered moving shortly after Robbie was born. The nursery decked out in Winnie-the-Pooh seemed to mock them. They wanted a fresh start. Elizabeth's reaction was a desire to pull Jordan out of school and educate him at home—to protect him.

But the best advice we both received in the crisis months following diagnosis was to *wait*, take a metaphoric deep breath, and get our bearings before intentionally turning our lives into chaos again. For Elizabeth's self-preservation and Jordan's self-esteem, the best choice was to make no immediate changes in his schooling. After praying for God's guidance, Mary and her family decided to defer selling the house for a time. They recognized they needed to grieve and then grow in strength as a family. Three years later they felt the timing was right to sell their home. It sold in four days. As always, the Lord's timing is perfect.

Any change in your life produces stress. Even "good" things such as a job promotion, a vacation, a new marriage, or a new baby cause stress. If too many stresses accumulate in a short amount of time, you can become overloaded emotionally and lose your ability to think objectively and make wise decisions. Most counselors agree: Don't make any life-altering decisions during your Year of Firsts. If at all possible wait, pray, seek wise counsel, and let the Lord open doors at His timing.

3

MARY

When Robbie was first diagnosed with his heart defect, I raged against God, against my family, against my friends, against strangers. It's a wonder I had any friends left by the time I was done ranting and raving and spewing bitter words everywhere. I felt like a blender turned on full blast without a lid to contain it all. Once the emotions were set free, I didn't want to turn off the motor. Nothing was right, everything was wrong. I viewed everything through a haze of fatalism. God obviously hated me, my marriage was doomed to fail, my child would never be "normal," and even my dog would probably die. I was a pitiful mess.

WHEN YOU'RE MAD AT GOD

But if it were I, I would appeal to God;
I would lay my cause before him.
He performs wonders that cannot be fathomed.

JOB 5:8-9

Most often when a crisis hits, we respond with a gut-wrenching, knee-jerk reaction. It's an internal response to an external threat. We get downright angry. "How could this happen? How dare the Lord mess up my life!" Sometimes guilt creeps in and we ask, "Was this my fault? What did I do wrong to displease God?"

Job was a man who had a right to be mad at God. He asked these same questions, expressing anger, frustration, and uncertainty. In Job 7:11, 20 he cries out, "Therefore I will not keep silent; I will speak out in the anguish of my spirit, I will complain in the bitterness of my soul. . . . Why have you made me your target? Have I become a burden to you?"

It's important to allow yourself these agonizing feelings. God gave us the ability to feel pain as well as joy, to cry as well as to laugh. He created us as emotional beings. Just look at the pendulum swing of emotions David communicates throughout the Psalms! Suppression of emotion is a denial of the human spirit that God gave to each one of us and can lead to physical problems. Unexpressed anger is one of the causes of depression.

Many people erroneously think we are not "allowed" to be angry at God. Our personal belief is that anger is a justifiable emotion, but dangerous. It is justifiable because sometimes it motivates us to a positive response (for example, when people feel angry at an injustice, it motivates them to work toward eliminating it). Anger is dangerous because it puts us on the defense, and we may express it with volatile words and actions. We have a choice to make—*react* in anger or *respond* to the anger. React by striking out against those we love, or respond by seeking a positive way to work through our anger. Do you see the difference?

Despite the undeniable anguish Job suffered—physically, emotionally, and spiritually—he defended God and His actions, never cursing God throughout his entire trial. Even in the confusion of his circumstances, Job never denied the divine nature of God, saying in 27:11, "I will teach you about the power of God; the ways of the Almighty I will not conceal."

As Job persevered to the very end of his long discourse, he concluded that he served a great and awesome God. We do too. And this same God is the God of Noah. He's the God of Abraham, Isaac, and Jacob. He's the God of Moses.

Our God, who brought the Israelites out of slavery and eventually brought them into the Promised Land, is the *same* God who leads you in your personal wilderness experiences. But perhaps our ever-present God seems distant to you. Have you found it difficult to recognize His presence in your situation? When you are hurting, is it hard to remember that the same God of miracles who took care of the Israelites is in control of your situation?

He *is* the same God, but He does work in different ways now. He's still present in an intimate way in your life and your child's life, but compared to His interaction with the Israelites, He may seem less tangible. Particularly as you're moving through The Year of Firsts and into the next years, it may seem that He's twiddling His thumbs in the backseat, carelessly watching your world whiz by, out of control.

Let us assure you though that He's still a hands-on God. He has not and will not abandon you during this emotional upheaval. "The Lord is righteous in all his ways and loving toward all he has made. The Lord is near to all who call on him, to all who call on him in truth" (Psalm 145:17-18).

LIVING ON EMOTIONAL "HOLD"

The initial shock of your child's diagnosis may have dissipated by the time you made arrangements to go home from the hospital, or the shock may still take your breath away for several more months. Even as you begin to learn about your child's condition, there may be an undercurrent of disbelief during the transition into this new lifestyle. You haven't yet reached the place of complete confidence in caring for your child and his condition. This is a time when you're moving steadily away from your old habits, patterns, and routines into a new, but scary, unknown wilderness. Between the old and the new, life may go on hold. Your emotional red light flashes, stalling you between disbelief and acceptance.

People respond to their time on emotional hold in different ways. For some, this place is as dark as the valley of the shadow of death spoken of in Psalm 23. You feel surrounded by towering dark walls, with no obvious way of escape.

Some people are void of any emotion. This is almost as scary as overwhelming emotions. You may think that there is something wrong with you because you feel empty, flat, like a deflated balloon. Some people even say the emotional emptiness carries over into their physical sensations too. It's as if the entire body shuts down, and it has forgotten how to feel anything—physical or emotional.

> *I was taking a walk a couple of days after Andrew came home from the hospital. It was a chilly day, and my fingers started to tingle. I touched them to my face, and it felt good to feel the cold on my cheeks. It seemed like I hadn't felt anything physical in so long. As I glanced down to pull the zipper up on my coat, I took a misstep. My right ankle buckled under me, and I sprawled headfirst across the road. Once I'd righted myself, I started to cry, as much from the actual pain as from the relief at feeling physical pain. It was such a contrast to the great emptiness that I had carried around for weeks after Andrew was injured. I suddenly felt that I would be okay emotionally because I could finally feel physically.*
>
> *Betsy—mother of thirteen-year-old Andrew*

For others living on emotional hold feels as if they're floating in a soap bubble—insulated against the pain of the situation. They may even be on an emotional high. When trauma is fresh, many people surround you and support you with prayer and their presence. Church families bring meals and offer to baby-sit. Friends call throughout the day to ask, "How are you doing?" A prayer covering enfolds your family in a caressing cocoon.

ELIZABETH

> *I remember how taken care of I felt while Jordan was in the hospital. People took over for me at home, which allowed me to concentrate on Jordan's needs in the hospital.*

The initial insulation of prayer and help feels so satisfying that it's hard to think it could or will be any different. But the time comes when your crisis lessens in other people's eyes, and you find yourself facing the future as a family striking out on a long and sometimes lonely journey. The emotional hold button has finally stopped flashing, and you're on the go again. You're ready to face the "now whats?"

"Now what?" you may inquire of the Lord. "You've carried us through this far, but how do we make it through the next months and years?" The crisis phase fades behind you, diminishing, and your feelings engage in the process known as grief.

THE GRIEVING PROCESS

Dr. Elizabeth Kübler-Ross, author of *On Death and Dying* (1969), is best known for her in-depth study of human grieving. According to Kübler-Ross, the natural human response to any significant trauma, stress, or illness is manifested in five stages of grief.

1) Denial and Isolation: *NO! Not my child!* Denial is a protective response to something overwhelming. With the shock of terrible news we assimilate information only slowly, in small pieces. It is only much later, frequently months or years down the road, that we realize we have come to full acceptance.

2) Anger: *How could a loving God do this to me?* Anger seems to be the hardest and most persistent of the stages of grief. It has the abil-

ity to cause people to react unreasonably, defensively, and even dangerously. A mother who strikes out at everything and everyone in her path to protect and defend her child likely is motivated by anger.

3) Bargaining: *Okay, God, if You heal my child, I promise I'll never miss church again.* As if we could influence the Lord with our empty promises! But it's an important stage because it's the beginning of shifting the focus from ourselves to God's almighty power.

4) Depression: *How can I even get out of bed and get through the day?* Depression returns the person to a self-focused outlook. Depression immobilizes a person. A depressed person may vacillate between feeling intense inner emotional pain and feeling completely numb.

5) Acceptance: *Not my will, but Thine be done.* Acceptance for the Christian comes when a person submits wholly to the Lord. It doesn't mean that we understand why the event happened. It doesn't mean that all the nagging questions have been answered. Acceptance means simply that the person has relinquished tight-fisted control to the Lord's control.

People who don't know the Lord or don't have personal knowledge of His divine nature can get lost in these stages of grief. Months and years go by without their coming to acceptance. They continue to grieve, be angry, and feel depressed.

Aren't you glad you can see the stages of grief from a godly perspective and know that even if you can't feel acceptance of your child's condition now, someday you will accept it through God's grace? "Then they cried to the Lord in their trouble, and he saved them from their distress. He brought them out of darkness and the deepest gloom and broke away their chains. Let them give thanks to the Lord for his unfailing love" (Psalm 107:13-15).

MARY

At four days old Robbie weakly sucked on the tip of my little finger while we waited anxiously for the doctor's diagnosis of the initial echocardiogram. In the space of half an hour I went through all five stages of grief. Dwelling a long time on bargaining (God, if You only make this awful thing go away, I'll never question You again), and denial (It's a dream; I'm going to wake up any minute now), I then took a deep breath and thought I'd prepare myself for the worst news imaginable: (There's nothing we can do—he only has a few hours to live.) I thought I could accept whatever was to come. But half an hour later when the doctor told us the truth about Robbie's condition, I was plunged into the beginning of serious denial all over again!

Over the next few years I found I went through the process of grieving anytime I was brought face to face with any issue or change in Robbie's condition. And every time I found I was thrown back into the turmoil of grief, I got mad at myself. Hadn't I accepted it yet? Hadn't I (just this morning, yesterday, last week) finally "let go and let God?"

The stages of grief do not come in a neat and tidy package with directions that help you proceed through the quagmire of emotions. There is no convenient step-by-step formula. Some people get really mad first; others deny, deny, deny; and still others bargain like seasoned bidders at an auction. All five phases can happen at once in short succession, or they may take years. You may find yourself thrown back into a phase over and over that you thought you'd overcome.

Grieving for your chronic child is an acknowledgment that your child will not be who or what you expected. That's painful! You're grieving the loss of your child's health. We all assume that our children will be healthy when they are born and while growing up. We may *fear* something going wrong, but we don't actually *believe* something will go wrong. When something does happen, we are surprised. This isn't the way we had envisioned it! We had plans for our kids!

Of course, we all have hopes and dreams for our children. We feel somewhat betrayed when we realize that those hopes will not come to fruition. What were some hopes you had for your child? Skiing together as a family? Gaining a college education? Working as a missionary? Becoming a minister? Giving birth to and raising children? Joining the armed forces? It's key to remember these were *our* plans, and no matter how right and good they seem to us, they might not be God's plan for your child.

PETER, JORDAN'S FATHER

Before Jordan was diagnosed with diabetes at age six, I some-
times would think about what his life would be. Maybe he'd
become a professional athlete since he seemed so coordinated at
sports. Maybe he'd combine his interest in airplanes and his
patriotic bent and join the Air Force. I even harbored a wish that
he'd join NASA and be part of galaxy exploration. But after
he was diagnosed, all those dreams vanished. Yes, there are still
many things he can do when he grows up, including sports, but
I had to consciously put aside my dreams for him. What it really
has come down to for Elizabeth and me is that we have had to
grieve the loss of choices.

You too may have found that in your mind you're learning to let
go of choices for your child. Loss of those choices seem to narrow
your child's world a little, or a lot. But when we consider it, the only
choice really is God's choice, and His divine will is for your child to
excel using his special abilities.

During the grieving process you may find yourself either drawing closer to the Lord for strength or pushing away from Him. One
day you may be in close communion with Him and rejoice in His
presence, but the next day you find yourself holding Him at arm's
length again. Who has stepped away? We need to remember that
sometimes the separation we feel from God during crisis times is
caused by our own reactions. We are the ones who have stepped away;
we are the ones who have relegated Him to the backseat. How? By
our own question "why?"

ASKING WHY

MARY

After flying through the first month on a wave of God's pres-
ence, I wasn't ready for the letdown that followed. After Robbie
was born, it took several months for me to even get to the point
of asking why. Living with a chronic infant meant that much
of my day was spent on measured feedings, droppers full of med-
ication, trips to the doctor for weight checks, medication dosage

adjustments, etc. Never mind the daily household chores, or my job, or the rest of my family. When I wasn't dealing with Robbie's needs, all I wanted to do was sleep.

I actively avoided asking the why question because I felt that if I searched for a reason behind it all, I might find that I wasn't being a "good" Christian. Also asking why implied that I was ready for an answer. It meant I would recognize the need for an answer. If I asked why, I would be admitting I didn't have all the answers.

Up until this time I had been very successful at keeping God in a box. I controlled my relationship with Him. I let Him only into those areas of my life that I chose to. Asking why would let Him too close and blow that box to bits!

The harder I tried to control all the events and emotions jumbled up inside me, the deeper I sank into a depressed state. At one point I even contemplated driving off a bridge with my two children. Wouldn't it just be easier in heaven?

It's amazing that I had such a distorted perception of the God of the universe! He is certainly big enough to hear His children ask why.

When I did finally ask, it loosened the thick cords of depression that had bound me. Suddenly I could allow myself the freedom to say without reservation that this was hard for me. I wasn't going to be the perfect Christian, mother, wife, etc. I didn't have it all together.

Have you allowed yourself to ask the why question? Many more whys boil to the surface once we allow the first why to pass our lips.

Why me?

Why my child?

Who do You think You are, messing with my child's life?

Are You mad at me, God?

Is this punishment?

Is this Your perfect plan for my life? My child's life?

ARE YOU THERE, GOD?

If you've had a tight grip on your internal questions, once these pass into your consciousness, your ordered world may seem ready to collapse. All these questions, though important to ask and have personally answered, pose a threat of unbelief. We believe it's vital to a continued personal growth in the Lord to ask thought-provoking, intelligent questions. But it's also a short step to disbelief and loss of faith. Psalm 73:2 expresses alarm over loss of faith this way: "But as for me, my feet had almost slipped; I had nearly lost my foothold."

We wouldn't be honest with ourselves if we didn't admit that sometimes we try to challenge God's plan. He's big enough and compassionate enough to absorb our questions, but we need to be careful to keep the questions from pulling us into the threatening grasp of self-pity.

Self-pity is just that. It's a self-centered way to look at your situation. But it's not *your* situation at all. You have been chosen by God to be the parent to a child with special needs and considerations. God will uniquely qualify and prepare you to be the best possible parent to him. Proverbs 3:26 gives us a promise as we grow into the role of parenting a chronic child: "For the Lord will be your confidence and will keep your foot from being snared." Growing in God's confidence will prevent the snare of self-focus. Self-focus diverts your attention from the Lord, from His saving grace. Paul reminded us: "You are not your own; you were bought at a price" (1 Corinthians 6:19-20).

How Can This Be Your Best?

Even once we release self-pity, there still may be a nagging question: "This is the best You could do for my kid? This is Your best plan?"

That's right. This is the Lord's best plan for your child. It's not Plan B, it's not "the alternative," it's not a mistake.

ELIZABETH

> One of my first questions to the Lord was how could this possibly be God's best for Jordan? How could this dangerous, eventually fatal disease be the right thing for a little six-year-old's body and life? We had prayed before and since Jordan's birth that he would grow to be a godly man and use his gifts and skills to honor and glorify the Lord. Wouldn't this disease interfere with that prayer of faith?

But therein was my answer. Did I only want the positive things of Jordan's life to glorify God—just his talents, gifts, and skills? Or did I want all of Jordan's life to glorify God? Was I willing to see that this disease was how God could best be glorified through my son? I had to be willing to relinquish my son to this disease if that was how God could receive glory and honor.

That's a tall order! But you know what? God knows what it's like to sacrifice a Son so that His glory will shine. God's best plan for His son Jesus was death on a cross. He *does* know the pain you as a parent bear in allowing your child's condition to bring Him glory. Do we have any authority to question or deny that?

Sour Hearts

When we were teenagers, our mother hung a sign in our bathroom: "When life gives you lemons . . . make lemonade!" As young women we learned to try to have a positive outlook. But that saying takes on a bitter taste when you feel that your whole life is one giant lemon and you've lost the recipe for making lemonade! And what if the lemon you're handed isn't what you were expecting, or you don't have the ingredients to sugarcoat it? Life with a chronic kid can leave a perpetual sour spirit in our hearts if we're not careful.

A sour-lemon heart is an obstinate heart. It's a puckered heart of defiance, a hardened heart of sin. This hardened heart acts as a barrier over our souls, blocking communication with the Lord. It is a stubbornness that in essence says we are trusting our view of the situation (it's unfair) rather than the Lord's.

Remember Job's question why at the beginning of this chapter? As readers we are privy to the conversations between God and Satan at the outset of the book of Job. But Job does not know about God allowing Satan to disrupt Job's life. Job's questions are valid! The key idea to note, however, is that God never fully answered Job. Instead He returned the inquiry to Job, asking piercing, comprehensive questions about the creation of the entire universe and the very nature of God Himself: "Brace yourself like a man; I will question you, and you shall answer me" (Job 38:3). Job became seriously repentant once he recognized the error of demanding an answer to his why. "I know that you can do all things; no plan of yours can be thwarted. . . . My ears had heard of you but now my eyes have seen you. Therefore I despise myself and repent in dust and ashes" (Job 42:2, 5-6).

Isaiah 30 addresses the ever-present issue of humanity's stubborn tendency to ask why. "'Woe to the obstinate children,' declares the Lord, 'to those who carry out plans that are not mine, forming an alliance, but not by my Spirit" (v. 1). Then the Lord levels a serious charge at those guilty of the sin of sour hearts: "Because you have rejected this message, relied on oppression and depended on deceit, this sin will become for you like a high wall, cracked and bulging, that collapses suddenly, in an instant. It will break in pieces like pottery, shattered so mercilessly that among its pieces not a fragment will be found for taking coals from a hearth or scooping water out of a cistern" (vv. 12-14).

Imagine your various why questions, which have possibly turned your heart sour, as a wall separating you from God. It's a high, ivy-covered wall, cracked and bulging. A mere touch, a tiny breath from the Lord will collapse that wall. He wants to eradicate those questions that have separated you from Him. His grace mercifully shatters the wall. He does this so completely that there isn't a piece big enough left for the dust of the whys to gather.

We know this is true and this is what He desires because the verses following 12-14 are filled with His words of compassion and promise: "In repentance and rest is your salvation, in quietness and trust is your strength. . . . Yet the Lord longs to be gracious to you; he rises to show you compassion. For the Lord is a God of justice. Blessed are all who wait for him!" (vv. 15, 18).

It takes a tremendous amount of trust to allow God to smash the wall of whys. When it does tumble, we are left face to face with the One who can help us sweep away the pieces and answer our questions. The answers will always return us to the most basic level of our relationship with the Lord. He responds to our question why with His own question: "Do you trust Me? Will you trust the One who created all life, who ordained everything from beginning to end, who sees across the entire world, solar system, galaxy, and universe? Who has a plan and purpose in everything created? Will you trust Me?"

THE CERTAINTY OF GOD'S PROMISE

El Shaddai means "All Sufficient One." Can we trust the One who offers all sufficiency? There is really a deeper question here—is God worthy of our trust? How do we know that God is honest and cannot lie when He says He is trustworthy?

For God to be able to lie, He would have to be deceptive. He would have to sin. The very nature of God prevents this possibility. We shouldn't even write the words *God* and *sin* next to each other, because they are opposites. Like negative magnets, or the east and the west, or the North and South Poles, they cannot meet. They will never be compatible. By God's righteousness, His holiness, His purity, His blamelessness, He holds all certainty securely in His hands. Otherwise He wouldn't be God! "He is the Rock, his works are perfect, and all his ways are just. A faithful God who does no wrong, upright and just is he" (Deuteronomy 32:4).

We swear by His name in trust. In the highest court of law in the land, in whose name do we swear to tell the truth? God's. In marriage, in whose name do we offer our pledge? God's. Even our currency claims the conviction: "In God we trust." He is trustworthy, or else we wouldn't swear by His name. He is trustworthy. "Not *one word* has failed of all the good promises he gave through his servant Moses" (1 Kings 8:56, italics added).

Yes, sometimes the pain we feel about our children threatens to squeeze the very life from us. But that is the time to cling to God's gracious promises. Go through Psalms and write out as many promises as you can find and memorize them. Repeat them over and over to yourself. Live from promise to promise. If you feel yourself falling into self-pity, repeatedly asking why, or allowing a hard heart to sour your perspective, recite this verse: "Although the Lord gives you the bread of adversity and the water of affliction, your teachers will be hidden no more; with your own eyes you will see them. Whether you turn to the right or to the left, your ears will hear a voice behind you, saying, 'This is the way; walk in it'" (Isaiah 30:20-21).

This is the way, walk in it.

This is the way, walk in it.

The same way the Israelites followed their trustworthy Guide. Walk in it. Though you may not understand, can't fully fathom the reasons why, or struggle with the long-term implications of your child's chronic condition, the Lord has said, "This is My way, My best plan. Join Me. Walk in it."

PRACTICAL MATTERS

You might find it helpful to take some specific action when you find yourself repeating the various stages of grief.

During Denial: Recite your child's diagnosis over and over. Write it down. Call a friend and repeat it. Why? You'll stay somewhat "stuck" in this stage and find it difficult to move through the other stages if you haven't yet accepted the reality of the condition.

During Anger: Do something physically creative or safely aggressive—finger-paint in bright colors, punch pillows, pound on the piano, go into the woods and scream.

During Bargaining: Write out a promise to yourself and the Lord—something you can and will do regardless of the outcome of your child's diagnosis. It might be memorizing a specific verse or rereading a chapter in a favorite comforting book.

During Depression: Buy yourself fresh flowers (have a jar of change collecting specifically for these times). Go to a bookstore and give yourself an hour to browse. Find a creative project small enough to complete in a short time (even baking bread) to give yourself a feeling of accomplishment. Eat chocolate!

Reaching Acceptance: Record your feelings and emotions in your journal. Mark the date on your calendar. Return to the journal entry when you find yourself retracing the steps of grief.

Suggested Reading
   Trusting God by Jerry Bridges
   A Shepherd Looks at Psalm 23 by Philip Keller

4

When I started praying for healing for Caitlyn, while she was a baby, it was tentative, as if I didn't have the right to ask. I didn't want to ask for something outside of God's will. Then the more I understood the complexity of healing, that it wasn't about what I thought healing should be, the more I was able to let God work through my child. I could accept God's answer of "not now" for physical healing.

After several years of more confident prayers, I began to understand that His plan for her to grow up emotionally through her disease was a form of healing I hadn't thought of.

Lois—mother of twelve-year-old Caitlyn with cystic fibrosis

PRAYING FOR HEALING

But for you who revere my name, the sun of righteousness
will rise with healing in its wings. And you will go out
and leap like calves released from the stall.

MALACHI 4:2

God can heal your child. That part's easy. Of course, God has the ability to heal—He is a God of miracles, evidenced over and over in both the Old and New Testaments. We know He can, but frequently He doesn't. Why?

Is it a lack of faith? Is it ill-directed prayers? Is it that in an increasingly fallen world, the reality of broken bodies is here to stay? Is it that in healing, God, mindful of our hearts, knows that nine out of ten of us would walk away without thanking Him (Luke 17:11-19)? Is it that we ask in a presumptuous way—assuming that our conception of a "healed" child is God's will?

Some parents go through the first few years of their child's condition praying in earnest for healing. Perhaps they take their child to healing services or have the elders of their church anoint their child's forehead with oil (James 5:14) or claim Scripture promises. Let us be clear that these are worthy endeavors, which the Lord may use to bring complete or partial healing in a child's life. And we do not want to diminish the importance of seeking these means if you feel called as a family to do so.

But in asking for healing, are we still in the denial stage of grief—does it mean we haven't accepted the diagnosis and prognosis? Is asking for healing a long stride in our faith walk, or is it a shortcut of personal desire?

Only you and your family can answer all these intensely private questions. What we hope to do here is to help you determine what you are asking of God and why.

WHAT WE COMMUNICATE WHEN WE ASK
FOR PHYSICAL HEALING

What are we saying to our children if we ask for healing from a physical condition? Does it communicate that she or he is not "all right," that there is something undesirable or "wrong" with him or her? That he or she isn't acceptable in this condition? That this condition has to be removed for you or your family to be satisfied, content, or happy?

We heard the story of a mother wheeling her daughter in a wheelchair through a grocery store. A stranger said to the mother, "Oh, what's wrong with your little girl?"

The mother looked at her daughter and asked, "Wrong? Honey, is there anything wrong?"

The daughter shook her head and answered, "No, there's nothing wrong."

What a great response! Neither mother nor daughter saw anything "wrong" with her.

The deeper, more important question under what you are communicating to your child when asking for healing is: What does your child want?

ELIZABETH

>*Several weeks after Jordan was diagnosed, an elder at our church confronted us, asking, "Why haven't you brought Jordan in to be prayed over?"*
>
>*My response was twofold. First, what would it say to Jordan—that I didn't accept him this way? Second, knowing my son's reserved nature, he would be very resistant to a group of people praying over him.*
>
>*I maintained then and still do that if God wants to heal Jordan, He can just as easily do it in the privacy of my home as in public. That would be more in keeping with Jordan's God-given personality.*

Your child may not want healing. She may not view it the same way you do. Maybe she recognizes the immense responsibility that follows healing. Maybe she's found God's comfort so real in her condition that she sees losing that security as frightening. Maybe she likes the attention and perks she gets because of her condition and has become accustomed to being "special." If she is healed, she'll be like any other kid.

It's important to ask children with chronic conditions how they feel about healing and if they want prayer for it. If they don't, as much and as difficult as it may be to understand, respect their feelings. It's your job to educate them about healing, relieve their fears, and answer their questions, but after the age of accountability the final determination should be left up to them. Maybe in their spirits they know that God has a plan for their life to touch other lives. Our emphasis needs to be on God's love for them, as they are valued by and infinitely precious to Him: "The Lord your God has chosen you out of all the peoples on the face of the earth to be his people, his treasured possession" (Deuteronomy 7:6).

DO WE HAVE THE "RIGHT" TO ASK GOD FOR HEALING?

Yes, most assuredly, we have the right to ask for healing. But sometimes we're hesitant about asking for something that might be outside of God's will.

When we are walking alongside the Lord (not running ahead or looking wistfully behind), we are in step with His plan for us. In that place of measured steps with Him, we can hear His voice and determine His will. His will is always that we earnestly seek Him.

What's the motivation behind our requests for healing? Are we asking for Him to be glorified through the miracle of healing, or are we asking for an easier life for our kids? Paul wrote about checking your heart for your motivation: "Do not conform any longer to the pattern of this world, but be transformed by the renewing of your mind. Then you will be able to test and approve what God's will is— his good, pleasing and perfect will" (Romans 12:2). Your mind is renewed in Christ. As you become likeminded with Him, you know

His will. Your thoughts are no longer controlled by what the world might consider "normal." When you've died to your own desires and relinquished yourself, then you will indeed be able to "test and approve" what God's will is.

His will may be to open doors for you to attend specific healing services, or perhaps He'll provide opportunities for people to pray over your child. His loving approval may lie in simply waiting on Him while your trust and faith increase. Maybe the healing He brings will be for *your* emotional or spiritual restoration through your child's condition.

Healing comes in many forms; it's not limited to our children's physical healing. Also it may not come in the timely fashion we expect or want. When we ask for healing, are we expecting an immediate response from the Lord, or are we willing to wait for His perfect timing? Second Peter reminds us that God has a different timepiece from us: "With the Lord a day is like a thousand years, and a thousand years are like a day" (3:8).

Proverbs instructs children and parents alike: "My son, attend to my words; incline thine ear unto my sayings. Let them not depart from thine eyes; keep them in the midst of thine heart. For they are life unto those that find them, and health to all their flesh" (4:20-22 KJV). What does this tell both parent and child? Study God's Word, store it in your heart, hold fast to the hope it offers, because God's Word will bring health. These same verses in the NIV end, "[are] health to a man's whole body." This is why we talk about raising a "whole" child. Your child is not just a body but a person with physical, spiritual, and emotional characteristics.

THREE TYPES OF HEALING

We can say with confidence that God will bring healing to your child, yourself, your family. He does want us whole; He does want us free of bondages. He does want us to direct all our attention toward Him, not to what holds us captive.

The form of healing He uses may not be exactly what we were expecting, however. Is what we consider "healed" the same as what

God considers healed? Are we asking only for physical healing? God created us as more than just bodies. He also made us emotional beings with spiritual souls. Consequently, there are really three types of healing—physical, emotional, and spiritual.

Emotional Healing

Emotional healing comes after release from a bondage of some sort. That bondage may have been in the form of addictions, sinful patterns of behavior, or stunted emotional growth.

We tend to think of bondages as only adult problems, because it seems it should take years to develop the dependent cycles that lead to bondage. But the truth is, our children can be in emotional bondage too. Inadvertently we lead them right into unhealthy patterns—overeating to feed insecurities or loneliness, over-the-counter medicines to numb pain (internal and external), or "I can't" or "I won't" attitudes.

As the youngest of six brothers and sisters, Caitlyn had always felt like an afterthought. She was ten years younger than her next-in-line brother. I was tired. I had thought I was done having children. Then she came along. I allowed her to get away with things I wouldn't have permitted with my older children. Maybe I was trying to make up for the difficulty she had living with cystic fibrosis. But then I realized that her independent streak was actually a response to her feelings of rejection. What it came down to was that I hadn't developed a relationship with her. Even though I had been her primary caregiver, I never took the time to know her.

Because she had felt rejected all her young life, she rejected anyone who tried to get close to her. As I prayed for physical healing for her, I realized that the healing the Lord was performing in her was not going to be physical but emotional. Her own walls of rejection started to crumble, and as they did, our relationship grew and developed. I see that now she is warmer toward others and more tolerant of their differences.

Lois—mother of Caitlyn

Spiritual Healing

Children have spirits that are capable of communing with the Lord. But they sometimes also have wounded spirits that make them vulnerable to insecurity. The nature of these wounds depend largely on what they've been exposed to in their young lives. Older children may have spirits of anger pulling at their hearts. Younger children may have a spirit of rebellion or defiance. Even babies can have tendencies, which may have developed while they were in the womb, from early exposure to hostile environments.

> *Our son was eight months old when we adopted him. All we knew about him was that he had been in a foster home most of his young life. On that first day when I held him and he began to cry, anxiety overcame me. He thrust his tongue against the roof of his mouth and out between his lips. He arched his back, flinging himself away from me. I felt panic. I cried to my husband, "I think something is wrong with him!"*
>
> *As I laid him down to sleep that first night, I immediately began praying over him. In the name of Jesus I prayed against any spirits that may have been harboring in his little soul. I prayed against any spirits that he may have been exposed to. I laid my hands on him and claimed him for the Lord. I wept, asking the Lord to give me a heart for this son that He had brought to us. It was a long night. I slept only in the early hours at dawn.*
>
> *When he woke up a few hours later, I picked him up and held him. He relaxed in my arms. Immediately I knew those spirits were gone. Not once since then has he expressed any of the signs I had prayed against.*
>
> Chas—mother of four-year-old Ian

Physical Healing

Beyond the obvious healing of your child's condition, there may be other, perhaps less noticeable physical healings. Maybe complications associated with your child's disease have a delayed onset. Maybe it was the timing of emergency care—Robbie had an echocardiogram just as his condition began to turn critical. Or perhaps transplant organs or tissues became available suddenly. Maybe your child had an extremely quick recovery time from a hospitalization.

> *When David was five, we moved into an old Victorian home. We had some concerns about the age of the house, but we didn't consider repainting until David's lead count came back at toxic levels. Absorbed or ingested lead from paint causes brain damage. Yes, he already has impairments with Down Syndrome, and we didn't want his already limited capacities to decrease. We wanted him to live to the fullest as God had created him.*
>
> *We prayed for the lead to leave David's body rapidly and that he wouldn't lose any of his abilities. Two months after his initial lead count, his numbers had dropped significantly. What's important is that even the doctors recognized that the drastic drop could not have happened naturally. It literally takes months for lead to clear a person's system, and meanwhile it causes damage. David's functioning has not changed. To us, that was a distinct healing. No, God hasn't changed David's condition, but He did prevent more damage.*
>
> *Faith—mother of six-year-old David*

The question is: What will you accept as healing? Is your request for healing an all-or-nothing prayer? Do you believe that God will answer by granting either complete physical healing or by doing nothing at all? Will you accept what may seem to be a lesser healing in the form of emotional or spiritual improvement? Will you accept only physical healing and not the more important (from an eternal perspective) spiritual healing? Will you graciously receive whatever form He brings?

WHAT ARE YOUR EXPECTATIONS?

Another point to consider when seeking healing is how it will affect your relationships. What if God doesn't heal your child in the way, timing, or fashion you expected? Will your faith falter? Will you live with frustration? Will you feel guilty that you didn't have enough faith for your child's healing? How will the outcome affect your relationship with those who pray over your child? Will you doubt their authenticity or faith-walk? And what about your relationship with your child, family, and ultimately the Lord? Will dashed expectations cause you to lose faith?

Do you see how a quest for healing can actually lead to striving that becomes man-directed? It seems rooted in dissatisfaction and hopelessness. Our hope *does* originate and rest in our Lord God Almighty. If we believe that and choose to live by it, we stay securely fastened to *His will*. Then our hopes will not be dashed because our hope is in *Him*, not in healing. "Find rest, O my soul, in God alone; my hope comes from him" (Psalm 62:5).

If you do choose to actively pursue healing for your child, be clear on your motivations and willingness to accept whatever happens. Make a covenant before the Lord that ultimately all you want is His will. Say a prayer of surrender: "Lord, change this condition or change my perspective on healing."

HEALING MAY BE FOR YOU

It's through disease, discomfort, broken bodies, hurt relationships, and so on that we recognize our need for God's intervention—we see our finiteness and desire the steadiness of His infiniteness.

Once our perspective on healing is in alignment with God's, we are open to healing in our own lives. Maybe the healing the Lord has for your family is in *you*, not your child.

MARY

> *Shortly after Robbie came home from the hospital, a friend of mine asked me if I was afraid Robbie might die in the night. I said, "No, I'm more afraid he's going to live." My prayer was, "Lord, heal him or take him because I don't think I can do this."*
>
> *The Lord's answer came to me, not in the form of healing or death, but in the still, small voice He uses from His Word: "I will heal your broken heart" (Psalm 147:3). My heart felt ripped in two over my broken child, but I recognized that the healing God would bring would be for me, not my son.*

ELIZABETH

I found that while praying for healing for Jordan, I kept think-
ing of all the other children and families who struggle with dia-
betes. Was my prayer so selfish that I only wanted healing for us
and not for them?

Through various opportunities we have been able to increase
the public awareness of this disease. We have stood before
Congress with other diabetic families and relayed the importance
of finding a permanent cure for diabetes. If a cure comes, my son
will be healed. But I want the healing that Jordan may some-
day experience to include more people than just my son. I want
many people to benefit. So I pray for a cure.

We shoulder a tremendous responsibility when healing comes—a
responsibility to relay to others the glory of the Lord. God is not going
to bring healing of any sort until His glory can reach beyond just ourselves. Romans 8:17-18 reminds us: "Now if we are children, then
we are heirs—heirs of God and co-heirs with Christ, if indeed we
share in his sufferings in order that we may also share in his glory. I
consider that our present sufferings are not worth comparing with
the glory that will be revealed in us."

Is the fullness of God's glory worth the wait? Absolutely! Would
any of us want to diminish, prevent, or delay that?

The Gospel of John relates the story of Jesus restoring eyesight
to a man blind from birth. The commonly held belief in those days
was that tragedy befell people as a result of personal or parental sin.
The disciples asked Jesus, "'Rabbi, who sinned, this man or his parents, that he was born blind?' 'Neither this man nor his parents
sinned,' said Jesus, 'but this happened so that the work of God might
be displayed in his life'" (John 9:1-3). What was the "work of God"
Jesus was talking about at that moment? To display His glory at that
particular, precise moment to those around Him. After a cautionary
note that He would not always be physically present to administer
healing in this way, Jesus spat on the ground, mixed up a mud pie,
and plastered it on the man's eyes (vv. 4-6). It's a good thing this man
wasn't squeamish! With mud dripping from his eyes, he was told to

go and wash. What's important to note in this? Two things: 1) Jesus required an act of obedience, and 2) the healing wasn't instantaneous. The man's healing depended on his obedience and walk in faith to the Pool of Siloam (v. 7). After that the formerly blind man had opportunity to speak before the Pharisees several times, testifying over and over how he had his sight restored.

How about us? What obedience does the Lord want from us? What faith do we need to stride out in so that He may bring about the wholeness He has in mind for us, our children, or our families? And then will we gladly take on the responsibility to honor Him and testify to His glory?

The Lord issued a promise, contingent on obedience, to the Israelites when they complained about the bitter water at Marah. "He said, 'If you listen carefully to the voice of the Lord your God and do what is right in his eyes, if you pay attention to his commands and keep all his decrees, I will not bring on you any of the diseases I brought on the Egyptians, for I am the Lord, who heals you'" (Exodus 15:26).

PRACTICAL MATTERS

The beginning of healing comes in recognizing increments of restoration. By keeping a clear document of your child's spiritual, physical, and emotional journey, you will see advancement in character. This is an essential tool to use as you help your child grow into wholeness. It's a reminder he or she can look back on or you can read to your child as an encouragement.

With older children or in a Sunday school class, act out the events of the healing of the blind man. It becomes more real to your chronic child if he or she takes on the part of the blind person. This could have a profound, lasting impact on your child!

5

My anger was overwhelming at the injustice of the accident that caused Andrew's head injury. I'd never felt such intense hatred toward another human being. The woman who ran the red light said "sorry" and "if there's anything I can do . . ." As if that were enough to give Andrew back his cognitive abilities! I wanted to take the Scripture that says "an eye for an eye" and rip her eyes out.

I couldn't forgive her. Did she know what she had taken from Andrew's life? That he didn't feel "complete" anymore? That he felt like a freak? That he felt afraid to play sports in case he forgot the game rules, or his role, or how to catch a ball? His entire confidence was gone, and I couldn't accept the fact that someone was directly responsible for his loss.

Betsy—mother to thirteen-year-old Andrew

RELEASING GUILT AND BLAME

Let us then approach the throne of grace with confidence,
so that we may receive mercy and find grace
to help us in our time of need.

HEBREWS 4:16

Everybody everywhere will at some point experience health problems. It's a fact. Human bodies wear out, and sometimes God allows people to be afflicted earlier in life. We like to think that in our orderly, progressive world we will only experience those problems later, *much* later. We feel shaken when "later" becomes now. We think, *This isn't the way it's supposed to be! We're supposed to live first before we start dying!* Your child's health condition seems like a violation of the natural order of life and death.

Having kids is risky business. Risky because we are indelibly linked with their physical and emotional beings. Their hurt is our hurt, their disappointment is our disappointment. We are not only likely to feel pain and heartbreak over our children—it's practically guaranteed.

Even with progress in medical science and technology, diseases and chronic illnesses are on the rise. As shocking as it may seem to us, kids are not immune to this trend. Think about other families you know who have a child with some sort of chronic condition. Practically every family is touched by *something*—food allergies, learning disabilities, asthma, compromised immune systems, ADD. You name it, they're rampant. That's because we all have imperfections—physical, emotional, and spiritual. From the very beginning of our lives to the end, we are imperfect.

Originally, in the Garden of Eden, our perfect God created perfect people. Then those people fell, opening mankind to sin and imperfections. But God can take people with what we deem imperfections and bring glory to Himself. In your child's differences God's perfection shines. "Listen, my dear brothers: Has not God chosen those who are poor in the eyes of the world to be rich in faith and to inherit the kingdom he promised those who love him?" (James 2:5). James reminds us that what others might deem as unfortunate or "poor" produces faith enough to inherit God's promised kingdom.

Admittedly, some "imperfections" seem worse than others. As authors we can't personally know what it's like to raise a child in a wheelchair. We are certainly sympathetic, but we haven't experienced it. Nor can a person reading this know what we as authors embrace each day in our own children's lives.

God has entrusted you with the child that He thought would be just right for you and your family. He never gives us more than we can handle. First Corinthians 10:13 says, "And God is faithful; he will not let you be tempted beyond what you can bear." Tempted? Tempted with discouragement, tempted with anger, tempted with fear. In His faithfulness He will not allow these reactions to your child's condition to overcome you as long as you rely on His strength. That's honoring. He must think pretty highly of you if He's chosen you for this parenting job!

Even as you read the above words, do you know that what we say is true, but you can't seem to embrace it? Something is holding you back? It just doesn't fit with your situation? Maybe you're wondering, "But what if I feel I'm to blame for my child's condition?"

IS ANYONE "AT FAULT"?

Think about these questions. Where did your child's chronic condition come from? Is it genetic? Was it caused by an accident or mishap? Is it a "just because" disease—one of those conditions whose cause doctors can't explain? Have you danced around questions of self-blame: "Am I at fault? Did I do something to cause this? Is this because of the one time I took headache medicine during my pregnancy?" Perhaps other people have implied that there is a root cause behind it, possibly even suggesting sin in your life. Even if you know this isn't true, self-doubt may needle you, "Was there something I could have done or not done to prevent this?"

Both of our sons' conditions can be traced somewhat to family genetics. Robbie has a distant cousin with the same heart defect. Jordan's father's family is littered with type 1 and type 2 diabetes. Could we have prevented these conditions? No. Could we have known ahead of time with genetic counseling about the chances of these conditions? Possibly, yes. Would we still have risked having our children if we had been given definitive odds? Yes. If it was discovered in utero that our boys were carrying these serious conditions, would we have done anything differently? No, because neither of us believed abortion was an option. With these questions answered, it diminishes any sense of personal fault. We aren't to blame, but we now are keenly aware of the tremendous responsibility we have to raise our children free of any self-blame.

Accidents Happen

Yes, sometimes the Lord allows accidents to happen. His purposes are at least twofold: The accident gets our attention, and we then have an opportunity to glorify Him through it. Nothing will grab parents' attention more than a child's physical crisis. The child's very life suddenly seems precarious. The threat of losing part of this "bone of my bone" feels as though our own flesh is being ripped. The Lord has gotten our attention all right!

Your response is what He's interested in. Do you call on His name or turn away? He allows a crisis to happen to draw us closer to Him. Accidents and disease are a direct result of the Fall and the consequent sinful nature of all mankind. But your child's tragedy is the very thing that God will use to honor and glorify His name, as only a sovereign God can. Can we understand that? "Now we see but a poor reflection as in a mirror; then we shall see face to face. Now I know in part; then I shall know fully, even as I am fully known" (1 Corinthians 13:12). Paul reminds us that we may not be able to explain now why God didn't stop the accident from happening. Our knowledge or understanding is incomplete. We can't have the whole picture—matted, framed, and hung on the wall. All we have is a sketch of the purpose or reason. We have to trust that God will hold in confidence the full reason for us to know someday—maybe not until we get to heaven.

Joni Eareckson Tada writes in her book *Heaven: Your Real Home*:

> *This will be one of those fringe benefits not essential for our eternal happiness, but simply nice to know. The parents of the little girl paralyzed in a drunk driving accident will understand. They will see how her accident touched the lives of friends and neighbors, sending out repercussions far and wide. They will see how God used the prayers of people halfway across the country and how those prayers reached relatives and friends of relatives, rippling farther than they ever dreamed. They will see how God's grace cradled their daughter, forging her little character with nobility and courage. They will see that nothing—absolutely nothing—was wasted and that every tear counted and every cry was heard.[2]*

Self-Blame

The situation that led to your child's condition could be the consequence of choices in your life. We all are and will continue to be held accountable for our sin. But even if your child's injury or disease is a result of sin in your life, repentance doesn't repeal the condition. That's what a consequence is. It's a long-term, definitive reminder of past disobedience. Your grace opportunity lies in how you will allow the situation to bring honor to God in the future.

We don't want to sound harsh. God is a God of forgiveness, immensely compassionate beyond our limited understanding. First John 1:9 assures us that "if we confess our sins, he is faithful and just and will forgive us our sins and purify us from all unrighteousness." It's easy to embrace the "faithful" part of this verse, but we sometimes forget the "just" part. God is definitely faithful to forgive any sin that may have resulted in calamity in our family, but He's also a God of justice. Jeremiah reminds us of the potential of unconfessed personal sin to affect our children: "You show love to thousands but bring the punishment for the fathers' sins into the laps of their children after them" (32:18). That is a tad guilt-producing, isn't it?

Guilt

Guilt. Just the word alone can settle into a heaviness across your chest. Guilt is a confining weight, making it difficult to move forward. Guilt wants to grip you and strip you of your effectiveness in your parenting and your life—something the devil would very much like to see happen. First Peter warns of the devil's prowess: "Be self-controlled and alert. Your enemy the devil prowls around like a roaring lion looking for someone to devour. Resist him, standing firm in the faith" (5:8-9). The devil wants us weak-kneed and off balance. He wants us to feel so guilty we are unproductive in everything.

Yes, you need to take responsibility for any part you may have had in your child's condition, but then you need to move on. Getting stuck in guilt is like being captured in a revolving door: You keep going around at a dizzying pace, revisiting the same place over and over. It leaves you perpetually exhausted on all fronts. Pulling out of the dead-end of guilt frees you to care wholeheartedly for your child. Which does your child need more—a parent stuck in the cycle of guilt or an emotionally healthy caregiver?

Some guilt is good. It's there as a red flag from the indwelling Holy Sprit to warn us of sin or inappropriate actions in our lives. However, after confession and repentance, guilt has no place. Guilt is productive only for the amount of time it takes to confess sin and repent of behavior. After that, guilt serves no useful function. But you might ask, if I've confessed my sin and believe that I've been forgiven, why do I still feel guilty?

Sometimes the "feeling" of being forgiven in our hearts needs to catch up with our knowledge of our forgiveness. It's like playing emotional "Mother May I?" It can be a three-steps-forward, two-steps-back process. A conscious choice needs to be made: Choose to believe. Choose to hold your ground and not be knocked back by guilt. You may not feel it all the time, but believe it anyway. We can be assured that once forgiveness has been requested of our Lord, our relationship with Him is restored.

If you are haunted by the ghost of false guilt, memorize Colossians 1:22: "But now he has reconciled you by Christ's physical body through death to present you holy in his sight, without blemish and *free from accusation*" (italics added).

Blaming Others

It's our human nature to want to blame someone, *anyone,* when we think we have justifiable cause. If your child's chronic condition is the result of an accident or genetics in your family, it's easy to point a straight arm of blame and scream, "It's your fault!" Loss of your child's health feels like a personal violation, and you want someone to pay.

Is it our job to make someone pay though? And what would we do to hold someone accountable? If a person's unlawful action led to your child's condition, will the court of law find that person responsible? What if there is no legal vindication? Or what if the court of law somehow finds the person innocent and you feel invalidated? Are we to take retribution into our own hands?

The psalmist knew what it was like to suffer from seeming injustice. So many times throughout the Psalms he pointed a finger of blame at others, crying out to the Lord, "Can't You do something? Look at their wickedness! Won't You punish them?" Psalm 73 is particularly potent. "They have no struggles; their bodies are healthy and strong. They are free from the burdens common to man; they are not plagued with human ills. Therefore pride is their necklace; they clothe themselves with violence" (vv. 4-6). The psalm goes on for several more verses expressing dismay over these people's lack of morals and respect for God.

But then the psalmist has a revelation: "Till I entered the sanctuary of God; *then I understood their final destiny.* Surely you place them on slippery ground; you cast them down to ruin. How suddenly are they destroyed, completely swept away by terrors!" (vv. 17-19, italics added). The psalmist then rests securely, concluding that God will bring justice where justice is deserved: "Those who are far from you will perish; you destroy all who are unfaithful to you. But as for me, it is good to be near God. I have made the Sovereign Lord my refuge" (vv. 27-28). What did it take for him to reach this conclusion? Entering God's sanctuary, being like-minded with God, choosing the security of the Lord.

Should we pray for justice? Yes. Should we pray for personal ruin for those we feel "deserve" it? No. Vindication lies solely with the Lord. "There is only one Lawgiver and Judge" (James 4:12). How, why, and when vindication comes is left to the Lord's discretion and perfect timing. We need to trust the Lord to administer justice in His way, not ours. "For it is commendable if a man bears up under the pain of unjust suffering because he is conscious of God" (1 Peter 2:19).

And, yes, it takes a great deal of forgiveness!

EXTENDING FORGIVENESS

"If you, O LORD, kept a record of sins, O Lord, who could stand?" Indeed, we can't stand up under the weight of our own sins! Yet the very next verse offers relief, "But with you there is forgiveness; therefore you are feared" (Psalm 130:3-4). Unfortunately we have short memories. The immediacy of God's forgiveness doesn't necessarily affect our willingness or swiftness in forgiving others, although it should.

The degree of difficulty we have in forgiving others shows just how human we are. It is one of the hardest of God's commands; yet it is crucial to our spiritual health. Why do you think Jesus issued this directive as part of the Lord's Prayer: "Forgive us our debts as we forgive our debtors" (Matthew 6:12)? Verses 14-15 continue, "For if you forgive men when they sin against you, your heavenly Father will also forgive you. But if you do not forgive men their sins, your Father will not forgive your sins." How poignant!

Die to Self

Forgiveness releases you from *you*—from your human tendency to harbor resentment or anger. When we die to our old fallen self, we become alive for Christ.

How do we show we have died to our own tendencies toward retribution? Our heart attitude. The demeanor of our hearts will influence our words and actions. Are they words and actions of a dead-to-self, forgiving heart? Proverbs 4:23-26 reminds us, "Above all else, guard your heart, for it is the wellspring of life. Put away perversity from your mouth; keep corrupt talk far from your lips. Let your eyes look straight ahead, fix your gaze directly before you. Make level paths for your feet and take only ways that are firm." Are your spoken and unspoken words free from blame and accusation? Are you looking ahead to the future for your child and your family? God's path of forgiveness is a straight road, free from the litter of blame or guilt.

Modeling Christ

In the words of Jesus Himself, "Do not judge, and you will not be judged. Do not condemn, and you will not be condemned. Forgive, and you will be forgiven" (Luke 6:37). How much more direct could the Lord get? He came to forgive, heal relationships, minister to hurting people, and act in love. He expects no less from us as His ambassadors.

We have a unique opportunity to reflect Christ's love, compassion, and forgiveness to others, particularly if they are somehow responsible for our child's condition. There is a double benefit in expressing forgiveness. One, we've ministered an extension of God's forgiveness through our selfless act. But secondly, and we would argue more important, we've modeled Christlikeness to our children.

Our Christlikeness shows in a refusal to be swayed by what others would do because we are committed to do it God's way. This witness ought to be the very core of how we are raising all of our children, and especially our chronic children.

We can't mince words when it comes to the responsibility we have as parents to live our faith *for our children's sake*. Deuteronomy 11:16, 18-21 issues a word of caution followed by a command and great promise: "Be careful, or you will be enticed to turn away and worship other gods and bow down to them. . . . Fix these words of mine in your hearts and minds; tie them as symbols on your hands and bind them on your foreheads. Teach them to your children, talking about them when you sit at home and when you walk along the road, when you lie down and when you get up. Write them on the doorframes of your houses and on your gates, so that your days and the days of your children may be many in the land." That's a promise worth laying claim to for yourself and your kids!

PRACTICAL MATTERS

Partaking of the Lord's Supper is serious business. The symbolism reminds us of Christ's brokenness on our behalf. Communion remembers His supreme act of dying to self and forgiving others.

Discuss with your family whether any of you may feel a need to forgive others or release guilt for actions involved in your child's chronic condition. We recognize this may not be an easy family meeting. It might be helpful to have your minister or a church staff person present. After having a time of confession, share Communion with one another. Then remember these words, "The blood of Jesus, his Son, purifies us from all sin" (1 John 1:7).

6

My wife and I orbited in different worlds until Paul got sick with epilepsy. We both had careers; she loved to travel for her job. We wanted to be dedicated to both our jobs and our kids. In hindsight I can see that we wanted the best of all worlds, without a true commitment to each other, our family, and our children.

All I remembered about epilepsy from my college days was that when a person has a seizure, you don't want him to bite his tongue. My knowledge of Paul's disease was limited, let alone my preparation to parent him along with my wife.

We had huge, life-changing decisions to make. My wife continued to travel—I believed as a form of escape. We fought about it. I came to the realization before my wife that we needed to be either wholehearted in parenting together or completely apart. These have been the most heart-wrenching, selfless years of our lives as we made the choices to let go of our preconceived goals and expectations and create changes that we all could live with—together.

Lloyd—father of ten-year-old Paul

THE FAMILY UNIT

Then choose for yourselves this day whom you will serve. . . .
As for me and my household, we will serve the Lord.

JOSHUA 24:15

Every chronic condition, illness, or disease involves a child's entire family. Any condition is a "family disease."

Early on in a diagnosis it's easy to think in terms of how this will affect you personally and exclusively. Then your focus becomes a little broader, and you see how the condition will affect everyone else in your household. The problem is that it will affect each one differently. You can't expect your response to parallel your spouse's. If, as a couple, you are like other couples where opposites have attracted, you likely are so distinct in your responses to your child's chronic condition that it will be hard to believe that you're dealing with the same issue!

It's important to come to a place where you can all work together, even if your responses are greatly different. The health of your family unit is essential to the long-term health of your chronic child. We like the term "family unit" because it sounds like a whole product. It's the total, made up of all the individuals. The family unit is you and your spouse and children working as a group, *unified* in your approach to your child's condition and treatment.

OLD WAYS OF COPING

Nothing will accentuate your family's strengths and weaknesses more than a shared crisis. Whatever your family is good at will benefit you during crisis times with your chronic child. The weaknesses in your family unit will be exacerbated by your child's chronic condition.

In the past have you gathered together, forming a shoulder-to-shoulder alliance during stressful times? Have you leaned on one another for support and encouragement? Have you cried out to the Lord and knelt together to pray as a family? Or have you reacted to crisis by shutting each other out? Have any in your family become emotionally introverted during stressful times? Has communication been fragmented, leaving each of you silently brooding in your own thoughts?

ELIZABETH

I felt so lonely during the initial months after Jordan's diagnosis. Peter was present and even did much of Jordan's hands-on care. I did all the thinking and calculating, and Peter administered the injections. Even though we were working well as a team, I felt separated emotionally from him. We'd talk, but I couldn't share how much pain I felt. I knew Peter felt stressed; I didn't want to add to it with my whining. I couldn't cry in front of him. Being a Yankee, I tried to keep the proverbial stiff upper lip. I wrote in my journal: "God, I HATE this. I don't know how to do this! I feel lonely and alone in dealing with this!" I was using only my own resources to cope, and I knew I was failing.

One evening I blew out a candle on a tall stand we have in our living room. I wanted to be sure it was out so, tired and not thinking clearly, I tipped the candle to see. Hot wax poured over the melted rim and down my hand and wrist. I ran to the sink and blasted cold water over my reddening skin.

Peter rushed over just as I started to cry. No, not cry, sob. It wasn't external pain causing my tears; it was the pent-up inner pain. "I hate this, I hate this," I sobbed. Peter didn't say any-thing—he just held my shaking shoulders. But from then on it seemed that we had a meeting emotionally. I could cry in front of him. I could say how much I hated what the disease was doing to us. I didn't feel as lonely anymore. Sharing my pain with Peter helped me increase my coping skills.

A crisis in your child's life will test your individual coping skills to the breaking point. These acquired skills were learned in past trials. Have you faced personal rigors—perhaps a difficult childhood or premature loss of a parent or loved one? How did you endure those times? Did you fall apart, or did you flex your maturing emotional muscles and shoulder your way through it?

Your past has greatly influenced how you will cope now with the painful times of raising a chronic child. Take some time to think about and even write in your journal about some painful past circumstances and describe the outcome. Try to recall how you felt, how you coped, what helped, what didn't help. Looking back will help you see how well you are handling your current crisis and will help you prepare for future crises.

How about your collective skills as a family? Maybe you can cope, maybe you feel you're doing okay, but you can see that your other children are struggling, or your spouse has completely shut you out. We believe there may be a time for counseling in any family's life. This could be one of those times. Maybe your other children don't have the developmental maturity to express what they are feeling over their sibling's condition. Or maybe your spouse can't keep a grip on his or her emotions because of being stuck emotionally from something in the past.

> *Coping skills develop through practice. It's like being on top of a mountain, and when the rains come, you start to slide down with all the debris. As you go, you carve out a path on the mountainside. The path might be the channel for a shallow run-off, or it might be a deep gully. Once the crisis passes, you climb back to the top again. However, when another crisis comes, and you're forced to cope again, your path back down the mountain is going to follow that same route you used before. Thereafter, you're sucked along, following the same run-off route with each new crisis, until it becomes such a worn pattern that it's nearly impossible to fill it in or divert it to a new path. In the midst of a crisis-flow down your mountain, you cannot take the time to reroute, dig new trenches, or build dams. The time to develop new ways of coping is before a crisis hits again!*
> *Faith—mother of six-year-old David with Down Syndrome*

The initial crisis phase may have passed with your child, but do you have solid skills to continue to cope? Seeking help is a wise step for many families. It is not an admission of defeat; it's a request for a trained, objective person to help you develop strong coping mechanisms so you don't stay stuck in a rut. Proverbs confirms counseling as a good option: "The purposes of a man's heart are deep waters, but a man of understanding draws them out" (Proverbs 20:5). Let a "man of understanding" speak to each of your hearts to help you grow stronger as a family. A "man of understanding" can be your pastor, a family therapist, your child's doctor, or a trained lay counselor. Don't be afraid to seek help if you feel your family needs a rerouting of coping skills.

NEW WAYS OF COPING

We weren't created to cope alone. God created us as emotional beings who need interaction with others. That's why He created Eve as a helpmate for Adam. This first marriage was meant to be a model for all future marriages. They worked together as a team, they created children, they organized their home, they solved problems. But talk about having to find new ways of coping! These two had had everything provided for them before their mutual sin. Then they had to learn to provide for themselves from the earth. "Cursed is the ground because of you; through painful toil you will eat of it all the days of your life. . . . By the sweat of your brow you will eat your food" (Genesis 3:17, 19). That was a dramatic, new way not of just coping, but of surviving!

You too are being forced to find new ways to cope. Where do new coping skills come from? How can you learn them?

DANA, ROBBIE'S FATHER

When Robbie was taken to Boston Children's Hospital, our lives spun out of control. My family looked to me for certain things as husband and father. While I tried to be the head of the house and provider for my family, a lot of things were still at the mercy of the doctors, hospital, and my insurance policy. My wife needed support (but our communication was next to nothing).

Our daughter needed to be taken care of physically and emo-tionally. The financial aspects of staying in Boston (hotel and meals, phone calls and parking costs, along with many other incidentals) weren't included in our medical coverage. The expectation that I would get an immediate grip on all of this and on my son's critical condition seemed unfair. I wasn't given the time to think about myself or whether I was up to this crisis.

Communication

All new levels of coping are based on good communication skills. That's because coping is dependent on expressing yourself. Communication is not limited to just talking—it's how you relate with one another verbally and nonverbally. It's not just the words you say but your posture, tone of voice, emphasized words, eye contact, hand motions, and facial expressions. James 1:19 reminds us to use care when we communicate: "My dear brothers, take note of this: Everyone should be quick to listen, slow to speak and slow to become angry." James is suggesting that we be thoughtful in how we communicate and relate with one another.

We each have a relational style with which we express our thoughts. What's your style? Do you talk a blue streak and pour out every word imaginable, repeatedly? Or do you "stuff" all the words deep into your heart and just talk in monosyllables or grunts? Of course there are lots of styles in between these two extremes, but before you can effectively communicate with your family, you need to recognize what your relational style is.

In a book Elizabeth wrote, *Keeping Your Family Close When Frequent Travel Pulls You Apart* (Crossway, 1998), she discusses communication by identifying how individuals process information and then respond to it. Some people are Cup of Tea processors; others are Pot of Coffee processors. A Cup of Tea person gathers and integrates information quickly, similar to the act of brewing a cup of tea. Conversely, a Pot of Coffee person takes longer to filter all the information being poured in.

How do you respond then to the information? You may be a Volcanic Responder or a Lake Responder. You can probably guess that the Volcanic Responder has an instant, explosive, and volatile style! A Lake Responder has a quiet ripple-effect response style.[3]

These styles aren't right or wrong; they are simply the way God created people. Once you recognize what your styles are, you can have more tolerance and patience with one another when you talk. Think of your own analogies for how you communicate. The point is to learn to "hear" what your other family members are saying and then to respond in a way they can hear you too.

A great nonverbal way to communicate with your family is to start a family journal. Begin a journal by writing what you're thinking about, struggling with, or rejoicing about. Encourage the others in your family to write whatever they want to. It can be daily, weekly, monthly, or sporadic. It can take whatever form each family member is comfortable with. It can express emotions, it can be written as prayers, it can be Scripture verses. There are no right or wrong entries, this is simply a nonthreatening way to communicate. This is also a good way for children to be able to ask sensitive questions that they are shy about voicing. The point is to encourage each family member to "talk" openly. When each family member reads the various entries, it increases understanding of what others are feeling and helps develop tolerance of differences.

Another form of communication is to maintain a sense of connection with each family member when you're scattered throughout the day. In this age of many communication choices, you can find and use a system that will work for your family. Beepers are commonplace in the business world, easy to use, and relatively inexpensive. Cell phones work well in areas that have a good range. For families separated by business travel, E-mail and fax machines allow daily communication.

The reality of raising a chronic child is that you'll have emergencies at some point. Don't leave to chance how you'll get in touch with one another. Make a plan for emergency procedures and practice it to make sure it works. If your child is old enough, equip and train him or her to carry a cell phone or beeper. Each parent too can wear a beeper or carry a cell phone. Also, and especially if your child is young, carry all important medical information about your child on you, put a copy in the glove boxes of your vehicles, and have your child wear a medical identification bracelet. All these actions give a sense of reassurance and security to all your family members, and especially to your chronic child.

Building a Family Team

Your child, especially a young child, cannot treat himself, nor should he be expected to. Your job now is to equip him for his future, not force him to take responsibility before he is capable. Remember, your child has his whole lifetime to take over his care. Your responsibility ends when he begins to live independently. Even chronic children who will always need assistance will separate from you emotionally as they mature.

Right now, however, your child is dependent on your entire family to stay healthy. Siblings and both parents become part of the child's health-care team, whether they want to or not. Ecclesiastes reminds us of the value of working together as a team: "Two are better than one, because they have a good return for their work. . . . Though one may be overpowered, two can defend themselves. A cord of three strands is not quickly broken" (4:9, 12). Sharing the "work" emotionally and physically prevents exhaustion and the feeling of being overwhelmed.

Parenting a chronic child will be one of the most unselfish things you will ever do. Because you are constantly anticipating what she needs, preparing her for her future, administering medications or food or treatments, your family's focus narrows down to keeping your chronic child healthy. Everyone gets involved, and it requires a unified approach—a "three strands" approach.

Do you feel that your family is fraying at the edges as you have begun caring for your chronic child? In the midst of families falling apart in ancient Judah, the prophet Jeremiah relayed multiple divine promises to families when they stood together in unity. "I will bring them back to this place and let them live in safety. They will be my people, and I will be their God. I will give them singleness of heart and action, so that they will always fear me for their own good and the good of their children after them" (32:37-39).

What does "singleness of heart and action" mean to us? It is unity as a family in the way you will care for your chronic child. You will need to plan how to stay single-mindedly focused on not just your child's future, but on your entire family's future. Jeremiah reminds us that this unity is a profound witness to your children. Such a plan is a keeping of the faith in your family for years to come.

The unity required to raise a chronic child means working together as a family on the offense and on the defense to be prepared for any situation. The team understands what each player's responsibilities are, what each one's strengths and weakness are, and how to work together to keep the chronic child as healthy as possible.

Initially when your child is diagnosed, you don't know what you are supposed to be preparing for. You're just trying to make it through the day—you won't have a long-term plan because it's just too overwhelming. This is when you're on the defense. You're just reacting to the immediate needs of your child and family. Operating in a defensive mode may last for weeks or months.

But then you begin to go on the offense. You've seen the "plays" of your child's condition; you've begun to recognize patterns. You can view everything with a more seasoned, critical eye. Now you're prepared and able to fend off threatening situations. With the other team players of your family, you're able to meet any crisis that arises with strength and confidence because now you know how to do it!

In order for the team to operate at its optimal potential, there has to be a division of labor, a definition of roles, and clearly communicated expectations. It's like being in a team huddle: Review the situation, decide on a plan, assign tasks, prepare to be aggressive on offense, get in place for action, and then carry out the play. You don't just *feel* that you're more in control; you *are* more in control when you have a plan in place. You don't have to think as much because your course of play becomes second nature.

DEFINING ROLES

Everyone has a role in a family. Even without a chronic child, each member knows his or her position. Maybe in your family Dad works outside the home full time and is the primary bread-winner. Or maybe both parents work full time outside the home. Maybe Dad stays home, and Mom maintains a career. Maybe you split the housework fifty-fifty, or you've hired someone to do it. How did these conditions come into place? By default? More likely you talked about what would work best for your family. You looked at the schedules of your children, child-care issues, finances, expenses of working, your home, your vehicles, etc. A lot of thought probably went into your arrangements.

This same comprehensive look needs to be taken when you're parenting a chronic child. Do changes in your income need to be made? How about your home? Do you need specialized child care? Former questions need to be revisited, decisions need to be made, roles need to be redefined.

Once again, you're faced with needing good communication skills to answer these questions and address issues! It's helpful to write out what you see as immediate needs, changes, or serious problems. Then prioritize. If your child now is in a wheelchair, making the house completely accessible to him is a priority. If your medical insurance won't cover your child's vital medications, a second job or home business might top your list. When you break each issue down into what needs to be done first, the immediate needs are less overwhelming. The nonessentials can cool on the back burner. They'll still be there when you have the time and resources to do something about them. You can even write the nonessentials out on a piece of paper and file it away. Doing this may give you a sense of completion. Even though you haven't addressed the issues, you know they are part of the future plan.

Who's the Primary Caregiver?

One of the first roles assigned or assumed is the role of primary caregiver. Who will keep track of your chronic child's medicines, doctor visits, food intake, activities, special appointments, instilling discipline, educational information gathering, and so on?

Frequently this falls to the mother—for a number of reasons. Sometimes it's simply because she is home more. Even if she works outside the home, many mothers are still the overall organizers, home-maintainers, and schedule-keepers. Women are also uniquely gifted by God to oversee their households; just read about the Proverbs 31 ideal woman—someone wives and mothers can study as a role model. The third reason mothers are usually the primary care-givers is because of women's fine-tuned perception—again, a gift from the Lord. This intuition is what wakes you in the middle of the night before your child even cries out with a fever. This is the sixth sense that tells you something isn't "right" with your child before anything is even tangible.

We have a personal belief that this acute sensitivity is the way God designed women. It's not that fathers can't or shouldn't be the pri-mary caregivers—in a number of cases this works very well for fam-ilies—but women tend to have the organizational skills and intuition to juggle the necessary schedules for the family. Women who work outside of their homes find that that takes supreme organization!

We're not interested in adding to the bread-winner vs. the bread-maker debate. Our hope is that your family can discuss and recognize who the best person is in your family to be primary caregiver.

This is a lonely job, however, and that's why a team approach is so important. The primary caregiver is the manager of the rest of the family players on the team. Unfortunately, the caregiver also tends to be viewed by the chronic child as the "bad guy"—the one who enforces doctor's orders, administers medication, or has to say no to wrong choices. Again, the other players can assist with a division of the plays. Instead of Mom always taking the child to the doctor, maybe an older sibling or Dad could do it. Involve all the family members in discipline agreements and in carrying them out. Don't just tell your child you're working together as a team—show him.

Being the primary caregiver does require strong organizational skills. For some this is easy. For others it's a stretch. Work with your family to develop easy-to-use charts or daily planners so that all the caregiver has to do is put check marks in spaces. Enlist the help of other family members or friends to develop a chart on a computer. Invest in a large wall calendar to write down your child's appoint-ments. Even use a different colored pen on the chart for each child in your family. If you know your child has doctor's visits every three months, pencil in the approximate dates a year in advance and schedule the actual appointments as soon as the doctor's office has a ready calendar. This will help to prevent missed appointments, will show your child when his doctor's visits are approaching, and will encourage other scheduling to take place around the appointments. Even try to "cluster" appointments during the same week to give a feeling of freedom during weeks when there are no appointments.

Who's the Speaker?

Another role in team parenting your chronic child is the "speaker"— the person who does the talking on your family's and child's behalf. The speaker calls for appointments and has questions ready for the doctor. He or she is the one who expresses the family's collective remarks or questions to teachers, doctors, or specialists.

The speaker may or may not be the primary caregiver. We know of several families where Mom is the caregiver, but being shy, she leaves the talking to Dad. Talk with one another to decide who in your family is best suited for this role. Your family's speaker needs to be able to express concerns and questions clearly and concisely. He or she needs to articulate issues in a way the doctors and others will understand. Strong communication skills are imperative!

The speaker is an essential role in your family's team approach because all information will be filtered through that person. The speaker is the coach of your team, relaying information back and forth to all the key players. The speaker works closely with the primary caregiver to find the pattern that emerges from the charts and planners, which then needs to be relayed to your child's health-care team.

Family Rules

We all have rules in our families. They might not be written or even discussed, but everyone knows what they are: Put the cap on the toothpaste, lock the door when you leave the house, throw away the empty milk carton, pick up dirty clothes, wear a seatbelt, no food on the white couch in the living room. The rules are to keep your home orderly with everyone having some responsibility in household upkeep.

Raising a chronic child requires family rules too—rules that will keep your child safe and in optimal health.

ELIZABETH

Peter and I both like an occasional glass of wine in the evening. I particularly enjoy it after the children are in bed when Peter is away on a business trip. But we both realized this could present a safety issue for Jordan. If my mind is even a little muddled or my reactions delayed even slightly, I could jeopardize Jordan's well-being. My mind has to be clear, sharp, and quick to treat any change in Jordan's insulin needs. We agreed to a rule: No drinking alone and not more than half a glass together. It was another "dying-to-self" decision. The temporary, pleasantly relaxing taste of wine wasn't worth a compromise of Jordan's safety.

Just as the Lord issues rules for us to live by to protect us, so too we need to discuss rules with our families that will protect everyone— protect from hurt feelings, protect physically, protect spiritually.

Fighting fair might be one of the best rules you can institute in your family. Fair fighting might include no shouting, no blaming, no violence, no insults, no use of the words *always* or *never*, no fighting about your child in front of him.

The guilt a child can carry over what his condition is doing to his family cannot be overestimated. If parents bicker over treatment issues, diet concerns, or condition-related expenses, his sense of self-worth will plummet, allowing guilt to fill that empty space. Make an agreement together as a family about fair-fighting rules. Even post them on the refrigerator as a reminder.

What other rules can you think of for your whole family's safety and health? Take the time to list them. Get everyone involved so that the rules belong to all of you, not just to you as parents.

Start your family rule-making session with a brief devotional on how the Lord gives us rules for our safety and protection. Use the entire Ten Commandments as an example. Or 1 Corinthians 13 can be used as a guide for expressing love and respect to one another.

What will unify your family and strengthen you individually more than anything? A collective commitment to live as a family for the Lord. Your witness to each other and to those around you comes from the way you live out your faith amidst the struggles of raising a chronic child. Second Peter 1:5-7 suggests rules for life: "For this very reason, make every effort to add to your faith, goodness; and to goodness, knowledge; and to knowledge, self-control; and to self-control, perseverance; and to perseverance, godliness; and to godliness, brotherly kindness; and to brotherly kindness, love." Agree to make this your family's mission!

PRACTICAL MATTERS

Love is the glue that will bind you together with your mate. Some people express love through gifts, others through words, others through actions. Use this list to choose some ways to communicate love to your mate.

Send flowers to his or her place of work.

Bring home a single rose or a hand-picked bouquet.

Dedicate a song on the radio to him or her.

Switch responsibilities for a day.

Give her an uninterrupted hour in the tub or him time for a long workout.

Recite a favorite poem to each other by candlelight. Better yet, write your own to recite.

Cook his favorite meal; bring home her favorite dessert.

Say ten positive things each day to your spouse for a week and see what happens!

Send an encouraging card in the mail—just because.

Hold hands on the couch while you watch a movie together.

Suggested Reading

The Five Love Languages and *The Five Love Languages of Children* by Gary Chapman

Shepherding a Child's Heart by Ted Tripp

7

My brother was born with a rare heart condition. Sometimes I'm jealous of the attention Robbie gets. When he has to be in the hospital or have an operation, Mom and Dad get really worried (I can't say that I blame them), and they don't seem to realize I'm there. He gets prizes after shots and operations, people come to visit him in the hospital (ignoring me in the process), and one time he even got to eat brownies for breakfast! I finally told my mom I was feeling left out. It was better after we talked about it. Now if Rob goes into the hospital, Mom or Dad take time to do something special with me, and if Rob gets a brownie for breakfast, I can have one too!

A couple of years ago I suddenly realized the life-and-death situation Robbie was in. It really scares me to think my brother could die.

BROTHERS AND SISTERS

Blessed are all who fear the Lord, who walk in his ways.
You will eat the fruit of your labor; blessings and prosperity
will be yours. Your wife will be like a fruitful vine within your
house; your sons will be like olive shoots around your table.
Thus is the man blessed who fears the Lord.

PSALM 128:1-4

When a child has a chronic condition, it affects everyone in the family, especially your other children. Brothers and sisters may feel isolated, angry, frightened, or any combination of positive and negative emotions. Siblings may be full of questions, or they may completely shut down. They might act out or pretend to get sick. They'll scream for your attention when you feel least able to give it.

While facing all your other concerns, add in the dilemma of poor or nonexistent communication with your children, and suddenly you think, *I can't possibly deal with this added stress!* And yet you love them, and your heart-felt desire is for your family not only to survive this but to thrive.

A BALANCING ACT

You may feel like a juggler—tossing all the emotional, physical, spiritual, and attention needs of your family into the air and catching only the one falling the fastest toward a hard crash. This all happens while you're walking the tightrope of crisis.

Each child in your family deserves your undivided attention for a part of every day. Allow for special moments, even if it's just a quick hug and a "How was school?" You may need to schedule this time so that it moves from being a good intention to a reality.

During these brief times value each child for his or her uniqueness. Maybe one of your children is especially good at reading aloud; take advantage of that skill and ask him to read to you while you relax with a cup of tea. Maybe your daughter loves to help you bake or plan out a menu. Ask a younger child to draw you a picture or make up a song for you. Use Romans 12:6-8 as a guide for recognizing and encouraging your child's gifts.

Even in the midst of a crisis you can give snippets of yourself to your other children. Take a walk around the hospital with them, make a phone call if they are staying with family or friends, or tuck a note into a lunch box. All these things keep communication lines open and show them you love and value them.

Earlier we suggested reading Gary Chapman's book about "love languages." As he recommends, be sure to talk with your children in a language that communicates love to them. Does she like the outdoors? Take her for a walk. Does he like to read? Read a book together. Does she need physical touch? Rub her back or brush her hair.

BLENDING YOUR FAMILY UNIT

From your children's perspective, you are investing huge quantities of time and emotional energy on the sick sibling, attention they may think has been diverted from themselves. They may see their sibling's illness as the unwanted component in *their* life. Like a drop of lemon on their tongues, it leaves them with a sour aftertaste.

From your perspective, trying to parent other children and deal with their volatile emotions is probably the one element that could sour your entire family unit. Blending the different personalities, reactions, and emotions of your children is rather like cooking: All the components need to be compatible to make a palatable mix.

Salad Dressing Families

Oil and water don't mix. No matter how hard you shake them up, they never stay together. Adding ingredients or changing proportions doesn't help. They stay separate entities, unchanged by their interactions with one another.

Do you find that your children seem unable to connect with one another? As we all can testify, it's amazing how different our children can be, despite having the same parents. But there are also times when we as parents have unwittingly allowed a child to take center stage in the family. If a child has been allowed to act selfishly or has been pampered into thinking that he or she is the center of the family, there will never be a thorough blending.

What has your parenting style been? Have you established that you have the upper hand, with loving authority? Or have you allowed children to be mini-dictators, without boundaries for unacceptable behavior? Maybe you've unintentionally allowed emotions a free run because you fear conflict.

Self-centeredness is at the root of children's difficulties in blending. In very young children this is normal psychosocial behavior. But as children and families get older, those with chronic kids can't afford to have selfish children. Everyone embarks on a learning curve of give and take. Once again, it's an attitude of dying to self, letting go of one's own way so that others might be lifted up. Philippians 2:3-4 says it this way: "In humility consider others better than yourselves. Each of you should look not only to your own interests, but also to the interests of others."

What a salad dressing family needs is an emulsifier, something that can cause the conflicting oil and water to bind together. Christ is the missing ingredient. He is the one who blends the separate family characteristics together and permanently binds them. He not only unites families, but He provides a model for family members' behavior. The acronym WWJD helps children to think about what Christ's actions would be in a difficult situation. Teach them to ask, "What would Jesus do?" Even very young children can understand the WWJD question.

It's been said that a family that prays together stays together. Prayer is what will bring Christ's staying power and His perfect peace into the midst of turmoil and strife. Teach your children to pray for each other's needs—even if they don't "feel like it." We know that the power of prayers, even offered only half-heartedly by a child, frequently work to change the heart of the person praying. Modeling prayer as the answer in your own life will subtly teach your children about the effectiveness of prayer too.

Paul wrote in Ephesians, "Be completely humble and gentle; be patient, bearing with one another in love. Make every effort to keep the unity of the Spirit through the bond of peace" (4:2-3). Family unity is available through the bond with the Prince of Peace. Memorize this verse together and repeat it when necessary to keep peace.

Sloppy Parenting

What happens in your salad-dressing family when you mix all the ingredients together and shake it up with crisis? A big mess! Who forgot to secure the cover in place? Likely you as the parent. Your responsibility for setting the tone and standard of your family mix cannot be stressed enough. A chronic illness is no excuse for sloppy parenting! If anything, you're even more responsible to be sure the ingredients stay safely in the bottle, rather than spewing out everywhere. It's irresponsible to check out emotionally and not stay actively involved in overseeing each child's physical, emotional, and spiritual needs. Feeling overwhelmed by the chronic illness doesn't mean you stop being a parent.

Parents are responsible *before God* to discipline the heart of the child, putting biblical principles into practice. Find the root cause for bad or unwanted behavior. Learn to discipline the *cause* and not the *result*. For example, your seven-year-old slams the door to the refrigerator when you tell him he cannot have a snack. The root *cause* of the behavior is a disrespect for your parental authority that *results* in the slamming of the door.

Without discipline a child has no training to govern himself as he gets older. He cannot develop the ability to perceive and partake in what is right. King Solomon was but a child when he became king. Do you know what his prayer was? "So give your servant a discerning heart to govern your people and to distinguish between right and wrong" (1 Kings 3:9). Our prayer for our children and even their prayer for themselves should be for no less.

The Bible is our authority for family discipline. "For the word of God is living and active. Sharper than any double-edged sword, it penetrates even to dividing soul and spirit, joints and marrow; it judges the thoughts and attitudes of the heart. Nothing in all creation is hidden from God's sight. Everything is uncovered and laid bare before the eyes of him *to whom we must give account*" (Hebrews 4:12-13, italics added). Matthew 18:6 also reminds us, "But if anyone causes one of these little ones who believe in me to sin, it would be better for him to have a large millstone hung around his neck and to be drowned in the depths of the sea." Would you want a millstone tied around *your* neck? And the Bible says this is the better choice for a parent who doesn't discipline his child correctly! As God has entrusted us with our children to raise, we are accountable to Him for the job we do. That's something to take seriously, wouldn't you say?

Of course that doesn't mean we can't fail sometimes. We are human after all. Honesty will ensure fair dealings for every member of your household. Be honest when you sin and fall short of the mark. Children need parents who are real, not people posing as models from "The Guide to Perfect Parenting." When you admit your human failings, children will find you more approachable about their own.

Cake Mix Family

The cake mix family, as opposed to the salad dressing family, brings many different ingredients together to make a rich, delightful concoction. Here individuals bring into the mix their own special qualities. Each one adds something and heightens the qualities of the others. Without sugar sweetness would be lacking; without vanilla the cake would be bland; without eggs there would be no richness. Children in a cake mixture family have learned how to give and take. They've learned selfless acts, and they accept discipline from their parents as a means to their own integrity in Christ.

The Lord is the leavening in this family. He makes the total mixture rise under heat, fuse, and become a finished product before God.

Each person in your family has had a part in offering this pleasing product to the Lord. You've prepared and taught your children well when you can read this verse with a clear conscience: "Even a child is known by his actions, by whether his conduct is pure and right" (Proverbs 20:11).

MARY

> *A couple of years ago I did a Bible study on parenting. I paged through the Thompson Chain Reference Bible and filled a notebook with headings pertaining to family life. I started headings on dishonoring parents, contentment vs. discontentment, family strife, teachableness, lying, self-control vs. anger, and so on. Then I wrote out every verse listed under each heading. Now when we have an attitude issue with one of the kids, I pull out the notebook. They look up the verse, and we discuss it and then pray for a changed heart.*

A changed heart is really the key. A child's willingness to be taught and then changed as a result is ultimately building character and nobility.

DEALING WITH CONFLICTING EMOTIONS

Emotions are like fragile bubbles. On one hand, emotions can soar skyward in rainbow brilliance. But negative emotions drag one down into a quagmire or explode on all in the vicinity. How can we as parents help our children to express their emotions constructively?

Planning for Panic Times

During times of stress and panic, expect brothers and sisters of a chronic kid to feel left out, scared, angry, jealous, and disappointed all at the same time. Defuse the explosion beforehand by preparing your family with a plan to deal with a crisis situation. "Mommy and Daddy are going to be very distracted when Tommy has a seizure. We'll be focusing on him, and we may be very upset and yell for things to be done. But it's okay; we aren't yelling because we're mad at you. One of us will stay with Tommy if we need to call 911. If we have to go to the hospital, Grammy (a neighbor, a friend, etc.) will come and stay with you. We'll call you as soon as we can. When Tommy is okay, we can plan something special to do with you. Be thinking about what you'd like to do."

Siblings need to know they won't be abandoned, left behind, or forgotten. Giving your children a plan of action lets them know you're in control, that you have thought it through, and that their needs will continue to be met.

Positive Flexibility

A child who grows up with a brother or sister with a chronic condition learns to be flexible and to "go with the flow." Because of this ability, maintaining a routine every day when there isn't a crisis is especially important. Order means an oasis of peace during times of stress and crisis. Children appreciate order because it represents your love for them when your immediate attention may be diverted to your sick child.

But flexibility can be hard for a child if it means that because of his chronic sister's illness or crisis, you miss the school play he's been rehearsing all year or a championship softball game. Make promises to attend important events only when you are sure you can keep them. What can you promise and commit to? It may seem to take enormous effort to follow through, but it communicates to your other children how important they are. Siblings of a chronic child need you to help them find their self-definition; watching them "perform" in a school play or in sports helps to shape your relationship with them and their sense of their place in the family.

Are there ways you can compromise when both parents can't attend a special event? Ask someone to videotape the play and then set aside a special "theater night" at home when things calm down again. Maybe one parent can go to the special event while the other deals with the crisis. Find ways to problem-solve as a family, making backup plans for the "what-ifs."

Kids with chronic siblings may develop a maturity beyond their years. Early on they realize what's important in life, and they learn not to "sweat the small stuff." Often these kids are able to focus on future goals early.[4]

> *When my brother Paul was diagnosed with epilepsy, I realized that's what I wanted to concentrate on in medical school. I had always wanted to go into some kind of medical research, but now my future dream became focused.*
>
>   *Philip—older brother of Paul*

Siblings of a chronic child can learn tolerance of differences in others and thereby gain an understanding of the consequences of prejudices. They can develop compassion in the proper context without crippling pity. Their framework for understanding pain, promoting independence, and simply loving their chronic sibling, widens to encompass others they see with chronic conditions or physical challenges.

You can help your other children develop these positive attitudes. Make a list as a reminder:

Do they get to see more of grandparents, friends, or extended family as a result of a chronic illness in the family?

Do they get to take more time off from school?

Do they have a more flexible school schedule?

Do they have a heightened sense of responsibility or freedom?

Do they get to spend more time with Mom or Dad individually?

Actively watch for advantages of living in this type of family and point them out to your children. Help your children apply these discoveries to others around them with disabilities too. Teach them selfless love—ways to serve in the family and outside the family as well. "Be devoted to one another in brotherly love. Honor one another above yourselves" (Romans 12:10).

Nipping Negativity

Children can manifest negative emotions through nightmares, moodiness, inability to eat and weight loss, personality changes, and/or lower school grades. Any change you perceive in your child should be a red flag that something is brewing beneath the surface.

GENNA, TWELVE YEARS OLD

I feel that my brother Jordan gets all the attention. Sometimes I think that nobody pays any attention to me. So much of our life revolves around him—when he needs to eat, when he has a doctor's appointment, when he gets sick.

Sometimes I think that it's all Jordan's fault. Yeah, Mom says it's nobody's fault. I feel shuffled around when I have to go to my aunt's house or friends' houses, but other times I don't want to go wherever it is they are taking Jordan. I do get kind of moody about it.

Do you hear some resentment in Genna's statement? Bitter resentment is a devastating emotion which, if allowed to fester, can grow and become the root of self-pity. Self-pity isolates, causing a callus to surround the tender heart of a child. As soon as you recognize this emotion, talk with your child. Confront the emotion and rebuke it in the name of Jesus. As encouragement for your child to reject bitterness and resentment, have her write out and memorize relevant Scripture verses. Talk with children individually and as a family. Spend time as a family looking up Scripture about the particular character traits that can lead to a hard heart.

Conversely, tender-hearted kids can also feel guilty for having negative thoughts. Remind them that the Lord created us as emotional beings. The negative emotions are only sin if people act on them or harbor them until they lead to consistent bad behavior.

Siblings sometimes have a heavy burden of false guilt, thinking it was somehow their fault that the illness happened. If they are old enough, have them read through chapter 5, "Releasing Guilt and Forgiving Blame," or paraphrase it for a younger child. Instruct them as to the difference between "honest" guilt, i.e., the Holy Spirit convicting the conscience, versus "false" guilt, i.e., guilt placed on someone who is not to blame. The devil uses false guilt to undermine a person's confidence in Christ.

Fear is another emotion that can paralyze a sibling. So many of these chronic conditions that are overwhelming to us as parents will seem catastrophic to a child with limited understanding.

Is the condition contagious? Will I catch it?

What if something happens, and I can't help—or I make it worse?

What if I hurt him when we are playing?

They may not be able to put into words the fears they have. Playacting with dolls, Legos, stuffed animals, etc., can be valuable for younger children who may not be able to verbalize fears. Journaling may be an older child's choice for working through scary feelings. Offer answers to unasked questions. "You know, Linda, Johnny would love to play soccer with you, and you won't hurt his incision. The doctor said it's completely healed."

Value and Vent

A child's feelings should never be devalued. Kids don't have the capacity to be mature. They need to know it's safe for them to let go and rant and rave (within limits) when they need to. During a private moment with either parent, a sibling should be encouraged to say what is on his mind. Consider this a time of confession when he can say what he needs to without threat of being reprimanded. This is a continuation of the trust you are building in your children. You are approachable, with ears wide open to hear their story.

Also teach your children safe ways to vent. "Safe" meaning that how they express themselves will not in any way hurt or injure another person in body, spirit, or mind. Safe ways can include punching pillows (or screaming into them) or finger-painting with wild, bold colors on large pieces of paper. They can go outside and throw snowballs at a tree. Anything that uses gross motor skills (wide swinging motions) will help release tension and anger.

Give Accurate Information

By allowing your children to be "in the know," you can help dissolve negative emotions. Including them in the research to understand the disease, its prognosis, and the care required tells them that you see them as part of the team and that you value their input. Don't sugarcoat reality or withhold information from them; they won't appreciate your giving them false or evasive answers. Even very young children can handle the truth presented at their level of development.

When Melanie had her first severe asthma attack, we had to leave her at the hospital and drive home to pick up our two-year-old son Garrett from a neighbor's house. As soon as we walked in the door, Garrett asked, "Where's 'Lanie'?" I simply said, "She's very sick, honey. She had to stay at the hospital so the doctors can make her well again. Why don't you get Dumbo elephant. I'll pack your pajamas, and we'll go right to the hospital to see her." He nodded his head and toddled off. It was explanation enough for him.

Cliff—father of nine-year-old Melanie

Older children may feel more comfortable asking questions of others—a pastor, a doctor, nurse, or the chronic sibling. Make sure the information they get is accurate. If you know ahead of time whom they would like to talk to, give that person up-to-date information regarding your child's condition. If you find out after the fact, a quick call can confirm what your child has been told, and you can correct the information if necessary.

As Christians we have a unique community available for support, unlike any fellowship offered elsewhere. Finding those trusted support systems will benefit everyone in your family, especially if you feel unable to cope with the demands your other children are placing on you. Don't be afraid to seek out others who can help your other children get their questions answered.

INVOLVING SIBLINGS

Whenever possible include brothers and sisters in any care or treatments.

When David was given passive physical therapy exercises by his physical therapist, my heart sank. How was I going to fit this into my already hectic day? But the first day we tried them at home, his two sisters got right down on the floor with him. They had a ball! It became a challenge to them to see who could get him to giggle and squirm the most. His exercise program seemed less challenging when it became the highlight of the kids' day!

Faith—mother of six-year-old David with Down Syndrome

Give siblings choices whenever possible so they feel valued as participants in the decision-making. Do they want to go with you to the doctor's appointment or stay with a friend? Do they want to check their sister's blood sugar or get the snack?

Talk about the future honestly. If you have expectations of how involved they will be with their brother or sister's care as they get older, share with them as much as you feel they can handle. Gradually give them small bits of responsibility until they are naturally in tune with their chronic sibling's needs.

Carefully balance the responsibility you place in their hands, however. If you expect your other children to watch a chronic sibling, make sure they know when and what responsibility they have. Never assume that a child knows what danger signs to watch for. Always go over any potential problems beforehand. This can be as easy as saying, "I'm running downstairs to put in a load of laundry. Carrie, you're in charge. Call me if Millie starts to vomit, (has a seizure, begins to cough, etc.)." When you come back, transfer the responsibility to yourself again. "I'm back—thanks for watching Millie for me." This tells the child when the responsibility shifts back to you.

Both of us have older daughters, and our younger sons have chronic conditions. Our daughters take their self-imposed responsibility of "mothering" their little brothers a little too seriously sometimes. We need to gently remind our girls that when we say we're in charge, it means, "I'm the mommy—you don't need to be. Your brother just needs you to be his sister right now."

SHINING STARS

"Do everything without complaining or arguing, so that you may become blameless and pure, children of God without fault in a crooked and depraved generation, in which you shine like stars in the universe as you hold out the word of life" (Philippians 2:14-16). Picture your children as shining stars standing straight and tall before a crooked generation that tempts them to be depraved and selfish. This is the vision we should hold for each of our children.

It's difficult to instill this in our kids when they face a constant incoming tide of negativism. TV, school, billboards, peers, maga-zines—it seems that everything in society tries to teach our children to be discontented and self-centered: "I'm worth it," "Just do it," "You deserve a break today," "I don't want to grow up," and so on. Teaching them to be selfless means swimming against the current (or more like a tidal wave) of negative images and self-indulgent role models.

Once again, it's the role model of Christ we want to present to our children. We desire to see them exhibit a die-to-self demeanor, a heart for serving, and a contentment with their lives. "For I have learned to be content whatever the circumstances. I know what it is to be in need, and I know what it is to have plenty. I have learned the secret of being content in any and every situation, whether well fed or hungry, whether living in plenty or in want. I can do everything through him who gives me strength" (Philippians 4:11-13).

PRACTICAL MATTERS

A regular time of family worship or devotions will strengthen the bond in any family. In the family with a chronic child, it can make the difference between a salad dressing family and a cake mix family.

How about adding to your family journal a separate section for prayer concerns for family, friends, church, and nation? In a regular spiral-bound notebook, use one page per family member. Then go on to list extended family, friends, church leaders, world leaders, and so on. For encouragement write in answers to prayers when they come.

Resources for Family Devotions
   Family Worship, Great Commission Publications
   Leading Little Ones to God by Marian Schooland
   The Family Devotions Bible, Tyndale House Publishers

Suggested Reading
   Living with a Brother or Sister with Special Needs: A Book for Sibs by Donald Myer (not faith-based, parental discretion advised)

8

I know more about food, what's in it, what isn't, how to read labels for additives, colorings, chemicals, vitamins, etc., than I ever wanted to know! I think one of the biggest issues for me about Caitlyn's food sensitivities is that I had always loved to cook. But this disease seemed to take all the fun out of it—it seemed like such a chore to cook for her. I researched everything I could for about a year before I got excited about cooking again.
Lois—mother of Caitlyn with cystic fibrosis

EDUCATING YOURSELF

Wisdom is a shelter as money is a shelter,
but the advantage of knowledge is this:
that wisdom preserves the life of its possessor.

ECCLESIASTES 7:12

The whole process of questioning God, developing communication, and researching your child's disease does not necessarily happen in a linear fashion. These facets may be more like pieces to an intricate jig-saw puzzle. As you fit one piece here and another there, the defining edges take shape, and soon the whole picture begins to emerge.

The importance of knowing and understanding your child's illness or condition is paramount to reaching the stage of acceptance and surrender to God's perfect plan. It is our responsibility as parents to move beyond the denial stage and become informed "experts" in order to act effectively as an advocate for our children.

ADVOCATE AND ROLE MODEL

An advocate is someone who acts on the behalf of someone who cannot speak for himself. While your child is young, he is not going to be able to make decisions for himself. Ultimately, it is our goal to prepare our children to be able to live and work on their own when they reach the age of responsibility, but until then we must act on their behalf. For those who struggle with severe disabilities and/or retardation, the age of complete independence may never be reached. Part of acting as your child's advocate, however, is to help him or her to be as autonomous as possible.

In advocacy you become a role model of sorts. You need to be willing to learn about the unknown and even scary aspects of the disease. Notice the word *willing*. Do any of us willingly embrace the challenge of a life-altering event? Isn't status quo a whole lot more comfortable? But the Lord wants us to be willing to change, to be willing to step beyond our level of comfort. "Grant me a willing spirit, to sustain me" (Psalm 51:12). Like David, we point a finger at our own chests and ask the Lord, "Who, ME?"

Yes, you. Being willing to research and become knowledgeable about your child's condition sets the stage for your child's acceptance of her condition. You are acting as a role model for her future comfort level and assumption of responsibility for her condition.

> *When Caitlyn was a baby, she was diagnosed with cystic fibrosis. I lived with the "what ifs" for about a month. What I didn't know about the disease scared me more than what I did know. I decided one day to sit down with the book we had been given at the hospital and read right through the chapters about complications and eventual death. It was hard and terrifying. It did nothing to relieve my fears, but it did force me to take responsibility for doing whatever we could to delay the complications.*
> *Lois—mother of Caitlyn*

Information can be frightening, especially when it points out the tenuous nature of your child's condition. But foreknowledge can protect your child's life. If you know what the dangers are, you can instill the value of proper self-care now.

WHAT ARE YOU PACKING?

Gathering information and learning about your child's condition is like packing a bag for a journey. At the point of information gathering, you're still in crisis. Your mind is filled with confusion. You may feel as though you're searching through a basket of unfolded clothes to find what you want to take on this "trip" into the unknown.

What else do we unconsciously pack away in our bags too? Fear. Dread. Anxiety. Confidence. Bravado. Independence. These and more are the heavy weights we slip into the side pockets and compartments of our luggage. They are indeed extra, unneeded baggage. Before you can gather and store useful information, you need to be sure you're free of the extras that want to play stowaway and take up space.

We all gather information differently. You are likely an information gatherer, a practicalities planner, a denier, or an emotion stuffer. Can you identify with one of these types?

The Information Gatherer

This person researches the topic, goes out on the Internet, hounds the doctors and nurses with questions, pores over magazines, and can make herself a semi-expert in a matter of days. She is like an attaché case—full of little compartments, pockets, and zippers that can hold all sorts of useful tidbits of information.

The information gatherer has a tendency to immerse herself completely in the pursuit of that elusive specific knowledge, thus narrowing her outlook and denying the peripheral. She may try to increase her control over the situation without really gaining any ground at all. The attaché case begins to bulge with precious documents, the knowledge spills out at any time (convenient or otherwise).

The Practicalities Planner

This type of planner and packer is tough; his planning acts as a hard shell, thick as Samsonite luggage. He likes to have his "ducks in a row," and as long as he can maintain order and stay in control of the situation, he stays healthy emotionally. Inside his Samsonite mind he has straps that trap everything in place; every practicality and possible contingency is planned for.

The Samsonite personality tries to control the situation through routine and order; staying tough lacquers a hard surface over the tender internal fears and insecurities.

Both of the above types must learn to let God be the baggage handler, because if they are not able to fully control the situation (and who ever can?), their baggage becomes a weapon. Rather than using the gathered information for their child's benefit, the information is used to cut, hurt, or defend.

Head knowledge without the discernment to know when and how to use it can quickly become an issue of pride. Pride has no place when you are acting as an advocate for your child. "When pride comes, then comes disgrace, but with humility comes wisdom" (Proverbs 11:2). Stay focused on *why* you are pursuing information; it's not for the education itself but to produce wisdom for the benefit of your child.

The flip side of the information gatherers and practicalities packers are the deniers or emotion stuffers. They shut down when doctors give information, tune out plans of care, and have only a vague, incomplete idea of the specifics of the condition.

The Denier

The denier hides from the truth of the situation. "If I don't know about it, then it can't happen!" Information is seen as a frightening, long, and arduous trip, so deniers go into emotional shutdown. This person refuses to plan for the "trip" by forgetting to bring luggage with her. "Luggage? Why would I need luggage? I'm not going on a trip!"

The Emotion Stuffer

This person is a worrier. He thinks of all the "what ifs." Perpetually waiting for the other shoe to fall, he too shuts down or tunes out. He is unable to process any new information because his carry-on duffel bag is stuffed full of conflicting, useless emotions.

We all have tendencies toward one or more of these types—no matter how contradictory that may seem. And all four types have positive and negative characteristics. You may need to adapt your style to gain the best possible perspective as your child's advocate. As you begin the process of gathering and storing information, remember to be flexible. We can't contain all the knowledge necessary in our finite bags. God has all the knowledge. We need to do our part in being prepared and armed, but then allow Him the control.

Proverbs 10:14 says, "Wise men store up knowledge, but the mouth of a fool invites ruin." We can "know" all sorts of things about our children's conditions, but without the Lord directing our actions and tongues in applying that knowledge, it is useless—to ourselves and to our kids. Remember, we are pursing *righteous preparedness*. In God's righteousness, with accurate knowledge, we are prepared to build a solid foundation for a bright future for our children.

FORMING A DEFENSIVE PLAN

Earlier we spoke of players in a ballgame. Players are always told that the best defense is a strong offense. Think of your education as the best defense you could possibly have when you're working with the intimidating medical community.

Even though both of us have R.N. degrees, the weight of all the new information left us staggering. We had an added disadvantage in putting unrealistic expectations on ourselves. We felt we had to prove to the medical community in our own situations that as nurses we had the upper hand and a grasp of the situation. Some of our kids' doctors also *assumed* that our nursing knowledge exempted us from a need for information.

Not so.

We and the doctors forgot to take into account that we are parents and mothers *first*. Being nurses doesn't even come in a distant second.

There was no advantage in having previous knowledge of general medicine. However, nurses' training did prepare us for some aspects of parenting chronic kids. We had experience in problem-solving and had developed observation skills. We knew the medical lingo and could speak to doctors in their language.

What about you? What in your past has prepared you to parent your chronic kid?

Consider these questions:

What skills do I have that will make me the best parent in God's design for this chronic kid?

Am I a good organizer?

Am I a strong nurturer?

Am I a problem-solver?

Am I patient to the nth degree?

Do I learn new things quickly?

Am I a detail-oriented person?

Whatever gifts you have, God will use them. Take the time to write out your specific areas of giftedness. What do you enjoy doing? What type of jobs have you held in the past that may have prepared you for the skills you need now?

Once you have determined what your strengths are, you need to consider those areas in which you are weak or need extra support.

Do I tend to tune out when I receive "scary" information?

Do I try to prove to the medical community that I understand everything they are telling me even when I don't?

Do I push people away when I really need their help?

Do I get caught up in the "what ifs" game?

Am I intimidated by medical personnel?

Do I tend to want to put *my* needs and emotions first?

Take a moment again to check off items on this list or write your own list of the areas in which you struggle. Don't be ashamed or embarrassed. The Lord already knows what your weaker areas are. If you need to confess them, do so, asking Him in His mercy to forgive those that involve lack of trust, fear, worry, selfishness, etc.

When we acknowledge our own weaknesses, it only strips us of human pride. With this gone, Christ's strength can reclaim us. His strength is made perfect in our weakness (2 Corinthians 12:9). Trust Him to support you when you need it. Trust Him to strengthen you and hold you up when you are feeling weak and fearful. Visualize this promise: "So do not fear, for I am with you; do not be dismayed, for I am your God. I will strengthen you and help you; I will uphold you with my righteous right hand"(Isaiah 41:10).

FINDING THE MIDDLE GROUND

Christ will enable you to grow stronger in your weak areas and build you up even more in your strong areas. Armed with your written list of strengths and weaknesses, you can begin to find a balance where you feel prepared rather than overwhelmed. The power of the written words on your list is a great motivator. Think about how you are going to use your strengths to be an advocate for your child. Ask God to clearly show you how.

Paul said in 1 Corinthians 14:33: "For God is not a God of disorder but of peace." Think of your quest for accurate information as an orderly process ordained by God; disorder and confusion are not from Him.

Thinking back to the analogy we used of the luggage, let's put it in perspective. What can the figurative attaché type teach us? For one thing, it can teach us the value of research. For another, it teaches us the benefit of being an informed advocate. Let's say, for example, the doctor has just informed you that your child should have a series of hepatitis injections, as he will probably be having blood transfusions at some point. If you have researched the advantages and disadvantages of these inoculations, you can pull your notes from one of your many little pockets or zippered areas and make an informed decision. Maybe the doctor wants you to try an experimental diet, but you have read something about it that sends off red flags in your head.

Being your child's advocate means making the best choices for her according to the information you have at the time. No one is expecting you to know everything there is to know from day one, but it's your job as the parent to track down the information and use it to maintain direction *and hope.*

What about those of us who are the emotional carry-all type, who tune out, or "forget" to pack anything for the trip of information gathering? Try breaking down the facts that are overwhelming you until you can find a manageable piece. For example, does your child's condition require (among other things) a change in diet? Research just *one part* of that diet change, such as snacks or protein needs.

Also, don't be afraid to ask for help in those areas where you don't feel equipped. In both of our lives the Lord has put just the right persons in our paths to help us with specific situations.

MARY

When I started getting bills for Robbie's various hospital expenses, I felt completely overwhelmed by the sheer volume of it all. Also, I've never felt confident with bookkeeping. I have a friend who's a whiz at finances and has a lot of administration skills. I got her to help me set up a budget and organize my bills into manageable piles. Then the bill-paying didn't seem so daunting.

MEDICAL JOURNALING

The medical community—doctors, nurses, therapists, and specialists—will work together to do what's best for your child, but they can't possibly know him or her as well as you do. Subtle changes may go undetected during a routine examination.

Medical journaling is very different from the spiritual and family journals we have already talked about. Your child's home medical records are the practical aspect of your child's daily life. You may find it helpful to write out an organized daily plan if you have a lot of medications to schedule or special diet needs. Other records you might need to keep include his diet and eating habits, speech and language patterns, or a chart of bowel and bladder habits.

A spiral-bound or three-ring notebook will serve well. Keep in mind that whatever you choose needs to be compact enough to travel with you. You can divide your notebook into different parts:

1) Daily records
2) Questions and concerns for your next medical appointment
3) Emergency and allergy information
4) Medical terms you want to remember
5) Contact persons' names, addresses, and phone numbers
6) Insurance information

Many changes in conditions occur slowly over time, and the best way to track them for your doctor is to show the progression through thorough note-taking. Develop your own shorthand, and don't worry about grammar. Just a few quick lines daily will show progress and patterns over time.

WORKING WITH YOUR MEDICAL TEAM

To a large extent, your child's health depends on concise, effective communication with his or her doctors and nurses. As we all know, communication isn't just about talking; it's as much about listening.

Doctors appreciate organized and prepared families. With your medical journal you are prepared to talk with the doctor and get your questions answered. If you don't understand what he has said, don't be afraid to ask him to repeat it. Discover how you best learn and ask him to teach you in that format. In other words, if you learn best through reading, ask him to recommend books. If you need pictures, ask him to draw you a diagram. Take notes or bring a tape recorder to appointments so you can review information later.

There may come a time when you feel uncomfortable in your relationship with your doctor. Be careful of "doctor hopping" too soon after diagnosis. Just because she may be the bearer of difficult news doesn't mean she's the bad guy. We spoke in an earlier chapter about moving from defense into offense with your child's condition. The first year is usually spent on defense. It's frequently after the first year that families begin to think more independently and proactively. That's the time to consider any changes in your child's health-care needs.

ELIZABETH

> For the first year after Jordan was diagnosed, we continued with the health-care team where Jordan had been hospitalized. But we decided we wanted a more aggressive approach to his care in a research setting. After some information gathering, phone calls, and consultations, we switched to a facility 100 miles from our home. The drive became a nonissue when we recognized that the entire facility's level of support focuses exclusively on diabetes. We felt that they were there 100 percent for us and for Jordan's needs.

If you're considering a move to a different doctor or health-care team, or if you have a vague dissatisfaction with your current team, consider these "patient rights:"

1) Any patient has the right to a doctor who is a good listener and who makes an effort to answer your questions.

2) You have the right to a hassle-free appointment. Is there easy

access to the office? Does the doctor keep you waiting longer than half an hour? Does the office staff treat your family graciously?

3) Your child has the right to up-to-date treatments. Your child's doctor should be knowledgeable about new research and developments or at least be able to direct you to someone who is.

4) Everyone has the right to information about different treatment options and an explanation of any treatments and/or medications. You should always know if a treatment suggested by your doctor is experimental, and the risks should be clearly explained to you.

Put simply, does your child's doctor value you and your concerns, and does he care about the well-being of your child?

If you do feel it necessary to leave one medical practice for another, get lots of references before choosing someone new. Discuss it as a family and make a list of pros and cons. Maybe ask another family with a similar situation for their opinion, or ask a national organization affiliated with your child's type of illness to recommend someone. Make sure that your insurance will cover whomever you do decide to use.

Most nurses are teachers gifted in sharing information. You and your spouse may even be assigned one particular nurse who will be your primary contact person. Develop this relationship to its fullest. She or he will be your biggest helper, cheerleader, and resource. This person should be accessible and treat you and your questions with respect. If you have a conflict with this person, don't be afraid to ask for someone else.

Sometimes a social worker will be assigned to your family, or you can request social service support. This person can help you find therapists, equipment, support groups, insurance delegates, visiting nurses, and other services in the community. He or she acts as a liaison, plugging you into different resources.

Another relationship you want to spend time building is with your pharmacist. For questions concerning your child's medications, he or she is invaluable. Pharmacists can easily access information regarding medication, side effects, drug interactions, and dosages.

Federal law requires that they supply you with accurate and easy-to-understand information about any drug your child may be taking.

OTHER SOURCES OF INFORMATION

You have a responsibility as you gather information to weed out the unneeded and keep the good. It's hard to know in the beginning what information to get and where to find it. Start with your local library and enlist the help of the librarian on the general topic of your child's condition or a specific aspect of it. Even browsing in a bookstore can help you know which new releases to ask the library to get through the lending library program.

The Internet is an invaluable source of information. Any topic you could possibly want is at your fingertips. Be careful though. The information there is not necessarily accurate or substantiated. Unless you know that the source is credible, never assume that what you read on the Internet is 100 percent accurate. Any information you garner should be subject to the scrutiny of your child's physician.

Take notes on what you read; draw pictures and charts if they help you. You are right now studying for the most important test in your life. Not to worry though—this isn't a pass-or-fail situation. It's not as important to know the information as to know where to find the information you need. You need to know whom to consult, how to use information once you've got it, and how to record it so you can remember it later.

That process is not as daunting as you may think. Start with small steps. "Apply your heart to instruction and your ears to words of knowledge" (Proverbs 23:12). Starting with a definition of your child's disease, begin your research by thinking through the following topics.

Terminology

What medical words do you need to know in order to understand what is happening to your child? You don't need to run out and buy a medical dictionary; most information from books, periodicals, and pamphlets will be couched in layman's terms. Never be afraid or embarrassed to ask people what they mean when they use an unfamiliar word. Don't let them assume you understand something when you don't!

Basic Anatomy

It may be helpful for you to review the basic anatomy of relevant body systems. What functions belong to the different lobes of the brain, and from which one(s) are seizures originating? How is the blood pumped differently in a child with a heart defect than in a healthy child? Where is the pancreas, and what does it have to do with diabetes? How does asthma affect lung tissue? How does your child's condition affect the other body systems? A mental picture of the body area affected by your child's condition will help you understand how your child's body functions as a whole.

Medications and Side Effects

Most chronic children require medication at some point or even all the time. For some kids, medication literally means the difference between life and death. Some parents take issue with this fact, however. It's difficult to accept the intrusion of medicine in their child's body, even though they know intellectually that their child will not survive without it.

Try to get to the bottom of your feelings: Do you distrust medication? Do you view taking medication as a sign of weakness or failure? Or are you worried that you will give the wrong amount at the wrong time?

If you distrust the medication you must give, research why it must be given and what will happen if you *don't* give it. For example, review the dangers of the seizures your child may have if you don't give him his anti-seizure medication. If you view taking medication as a sign of weakness, confess those feelings to God, and then take time to thank Him that there is something available to help your child. If you worry about giving the medication incorrectly, set up a schedule and make sure you are comfortable with the different means of measuring out the dosage. Ask someone else to double-check your math until you feel comfortable administering it on your own.

Complications and Emergencies

Unexpected difficulties have a way of leveling "the best-laid plans of mice and men." In your research take the time (when you feel strong enough emotionally) to study the possible complications of your child's condition. Knowing ahead of time what could happen will make the possibilities less ominous. Prepare now for the "what ifs" and then pack your plans away in case you need them. God is ever faithful, and He has an ultimate plan, even in the midst of a complication or emergency. He is divinely consistent.

MARY

I'm one of those people who likes to have all my "ducks in a row." I have contingency plans A, B, and C lined up for any and every emergency. What amazes me is that inevitably the emergency that happens isn't one I've planned for!

An emergency can throw all your ordered plans into a tailspin. And yet as advocates, we must have plans of some sort. Keep your previously mentioned medical journal with all its information easily accessible. Your child should wear a medical-alert bracelet or necklace. Keep accurate, up-to-date information about your child's condition in the glove compartment of your car. At least two members of your family should have basic first aid and CPR training. Teach your other children how to access emergency help via the phone, and add 911 to your speed dial.

All the information you gather and all the plans of preparedness you establish are acts of advocacy for your child. But ultimately the outcome is in the hands of the Lord Almighty. He will honor the effort you have undertaken to care for your child, as you've done it to the absolute best of your ability. You are doing the job God has entrusted to you. Now trust Him to take care of the rest. He will be faithful to protect the investment in your child. "But let all who take refuge in you be glad; let them ever sing for joy. Spread your protection over them, that those who love your name may rejoice in you. For surely, O LORD, you bless the righteous; you surround them with your favor as with a shield" (Psalm 5:11-12).

PRACTICAL MATTERS

Set aside a certain time of day or one day a week as your "education time." This puts parameters around your learning. The benefit is twofold. You won't become consumed or obsessed with researching, and you won't feel guilty for times *not* spent gathering information. In other words, if you've set aside Tuesday afternoons for the next month to visit the library for research, then on Friday if you sit down with a novel, you won't feel a nagging guilt that you are not doing "enough" information-gathering.

9

Before it was determined that Jessie was blind, my extended family was unsupportive—almost to the point of implying I was fabricating my daughter's difficulties to get attention.

My friends tried terribly hard to be supportive, but they just didn't know how. And I couldn't tell them how either. It was painful for me to see how freely they were enjoying their children's development and know I couldn't have the same experience with Jessie. Because we didn't have a definitive diagnosis, I even had times of self-doubt, wondering if I was imagining everything. It was a time of great loneliness and pain.

When she was finally diagnosed, the doctor confirmed that she had a visual acuity of 20/400—meaning she was legally blind. I wanted to stand on the top of the highest building and scream in relief, "See, I'm not crazy. I was right!"

Margaret—mother of seven-year-old Jessie

WHEN FRIENDS SAY HURTFUL THINGS . . . AND THEY WILL

A gentle answer turns away wrath, but a harsh word stirs up anger.
The tongue of the wise commends knowledge.

PROVERBS 15:1-2

You've probably already experienced the painful stab of a friend's seemingly innocent comments. You grit your teeth and think to yourself, *Why don't you just plunge the knife a little deeper into my heart?* A number of sharp replies come to mind. You want to yell, "You have no idea what I go through every day!" You want to shock the person into understanding a fraction of what you're feeling. You want to lash out with your fists or tongue. You think, *Fine. You want to connect with me—here feel this!* You've been unspeakably hurt, and you just want to return that pain in multiples to the person who inflicted it— "friend" or not!

ELIZABETH

> *Initially I found it so hard to have any words of sympathy or comfort for an acquaintance who complained that her child had an ear infection and was on antibiotics. I wanted to scream at her, "You're complaining about the inconvenience of ten days worth of medicine—how it's interrupting your life! Try this on: A LIFETIME of shots, finger pricks, and food require-ments, any of which you mess up on, and your kid dies! Come live in my house for a day!" It took me a long time to develop patience for other people's seemingly trivial complaints about their children.*

It's inevitable. You'll be in the grocery store, or visiting with people after church, or at a social gathering, and suddenly someone will say something that rips at your already broken heart. Maybe what they said was supposed to comfort you. Perhaps they were offering advice. They might have thought sarcasm would help you laugh. Maybe they just didn't know how to be sensitive, and they blurted out the first thing that came to mind—something unbearably shallow.

It's been said that you find out who your true friends are when calamity strikes. Some friends just won't be able to cope with your loss or pain and will "abandon" you. Maybe because of a lack of their own coping skills, they don't know how to address you. They may not know what to say and fear saying the wrong thing. Maybe they're terrified. They have an irrational fear that calamity is "contagious," and you're the carrier. Perhaps they feel guilty for having healthy children. The reasons could go on and on about why friends will stick by you or drift away. Years later the ones with whom you lost contact may even come back to ask forgiveness for letting you down.

Think about this though: Haven't all of us experienced the thick tongue and jumbled words in situations when it seems impossible to put something appropriate into words? Can we really be critical of others for not knowing what to say to us? Proverbs 17:9 reminds us to forgive insensitivity: "He who covers over an offense promotes love, but whoever repeats the matter separates close friends."

Even as people who have experienced pain ourselves, we may still find it difficult to express the right thing to others. As we mentioned in an earlier chapter, we share a friend who has lost two sons to untimely deaths. In no way does our pain equip us to be able to minister to her pain. Both of us are at a loss to know the right words. Yet we're willing to listen and simply offer an ear.

That's really all we're looking for in true friends ourselves, isn't it? Someone who will just *listen*. James 1:19 says, "My dear brothers, take note of this: Everyone should be quick to listen, slow to speak."

THE SHORT STORY OR THE LONG STORY?

When people ask you about your child, what exactly are they asking? Do they want the whole story? Do they want a standard "everything's fine" line? Do they want the short story or the long story? Are they asking for their own comfort? Maybe they are asking to hear a testimony about the Lord's grace. There are others too, of course, who really do want to know every detail of exactly how you're doing.

When asked how everything is going, Peter, Jordan's father, answers with his own query: "If you want the short answer, Jordan is doing as well as we can hope for right now. If you want the longer answer, call me and we'll sit down for a cup of coffee." For some people this is all they want to hear: "We're okay." In that answer we've relieved them of any responsibility to "hear" any more, but we have left the door open if they truly do want the details. It makes them feel that they've shown concern without getting an overload of information. And it's freed us from reliving the story again or investing precious energy and emotions into someone who can't refill our emotional or spiritual storehouses.

OUR MESSY CLOSETS

It hurts, and you may be angry if your friends don't want "in" on your pain. Our human nature is to *want* others to feel our pain, not to drag them into depression but to share a common cross. Galatians 6:2 reminds us to support one another: "Carry each other's burdens, and in this way you will fulfill the law of Christ." This need to connect is an inborn part of human nature. And it is at the very core of God's creation of man and woman to complement and complete each other.

A friend of Elizabeth's calls cross-sharing during friends' difficult times the "messy closet" concept. Your confused emotions and your coping strategies are like a messy closet. What we all want is to have a friend stand at the open door of our closets, put an arm across our shoulders, and just look. We don't want the person to rearrange it. Or fix it. Or straighten it up. Or cart it all away to the trash heap. We just want the friend to see how messy it is! We want him or her to understand how much work we have to do. We want a cheering squad as we roll up our sleeves and get to work sorting through the clutter. Only you and your family can straighten your messy closet. But it sure helps to have a friend close by to offer a refreshing drink, a needed hug, a prayer of support, or a tender word of encouragement.

This situation presents a difficulty, however. The very people we need so much to be messy-closet-viewers with us are the same ones we push away when their response doesn't meet our expectations. But did you catch that? *Our expectations.* Some of your friends cannot view your closet. Something prevents them from being able to be objective and makes them want to slam the door at just a glimpse. You're left with a choice. Is it worth it to take the time to tactfully and gently show them, *teach them*, the details about your closet?

Only you can answer that. How much do you value this friendship? How much do you need this person to understand? Are you willing to invest time, energy, and emotions into educating him or her about the hazards you face?

USING THE WORD *NORMAL*

You've likely heard it already: "Well, is she . . . *normal?*" This bites to the quick. You want to come back with your own nip. *Normal compared to what? Is anybody truly normal? What are the parameters by which you judge what is normal?* A great comeback was coined by Patsy Clairmont: "Normal is just a setting on your dryer!"

What exactly are people asking when they ask if your child is normal? You might even ask them, "What is your definition of normal?" Unconsciously they are asking, "Will she fit in? Will he be able to function in society? Will she benefit mankind and benefit from our society?" Indirectly or directly they are inquiring about mental acuity. Our culture evaluates people's worthiness by looking at their accomplishments. We know our children's worthiness rests securely in God's plan for their lives. Children with disabilities can frequently accomplish more than able-bodied people because of their ability to reflect Christ in their differences.

There may be an even deeper question people are asking when they use the word *normal*. At the very core their question is, "Can he love?" and "Is she lovable?"

The answer is simple: God loves these children. They are valuable to Him. Christ died for them as much as he died for brilliant people with high IQs. "For God so loved the world that he gave his one and only Son . . ." (John 3:16). Christ's sacrifice is not limited to "normal" people but encompasses every single person God has created and ever will create.

So how can we answer? Yes, a child with Down Syndrome is normal—normal for a person with Down Syndrome. Yes, a child with cerebral palsy in a wheelchair is normal—for a person with cerebral palsy. Yes, the child with severe brain damage is normal, created exactly the way God could be most glorified.

Against whom do we measure ourselves and our children? God and only God. We can only determine "normal" by God's high standard. By God's grace and divine direction your child can develop to the full extent of what he can be now and will become in the future. How much more normal can we get than that?

UNASKED-FOR ADVICE

Just as a new mother is offered reams of uninvited advice, you too will likely hear from people who think they have just the right solution for you. People who know of someone else in your situation or have been through a similar experience or have recently read a solution for your child's condition think they are doing you a favor or connecting with you. Usually it's to make *them* feel better (they are the ones who want to tidy your messy closet), and they don't recognize their offer may actually hurt you.

Keep in mind that even if their comments are ill-conceived, their intentions are good. They truly want to help. But how do you answer them, especially when you know the information they have is incomplete, questionable, or even inaccurate? There are a number of strategies you can use. Smile graciously and say, "Thanks for your interest." Put the responsibility on your doctor and say, "Our doctor has advised us to stick to what we're doing right now." Or nod and say, "That's something to think about."

You can also take the opportunity to teach them a little something about your child's condition. You could say, "That's an interesting suggestion, but it won't really work for us because . . ."

ELIZABETH:

> *A few months after Jordan was diagnosed, I was telling a friend, who is strongly New Age and a firm believer in the powers of herbal medicine, about his diabetes. She asked the usual question: "Could he take pills to correct it?" Surprised that pills don't work for type 1 diabetes, she suggested taking him immediately off insulin and starting him on an herbal concoction. My heart wanted to scream, "Take him off insulin? Yeah, and watch him die in a few short days!" Instead I took a deep breath and literally sat down across from this individual and explained what type 1 diabetes is. At the end of my succinct but accurate description of the disease, she nodded and agreed that insulin really was the only option.*

Elizabeth had to determine if it was important enough to her to teach her friend. She could have just as easily walked away, shrugged her shoulders, and remembered that her friend was not approachable and was indeed even dangerous to her emotionally. Elizabeth decided that taking the time and effort to explain would keep the lines of communication open in that particular relationship.

WISE HEARTS

It takes discernment, tact, and grace to know what to say, when, and to whom. "The wise in heart are called discerning, and pleasant words promote instruction. . . . A wise man's heart guides his mouth, and his lips promote instruction" (Proverbs 16:21, 23).

MARY

> *Two weeks after we brought Robbie home from the hospital, we went to church as a family. It felt good to be "in public" again.*

After the service someone came up to me and asked how I was handling everything. Giving little thought to my words and assuming she really wanted the story, I launched right in. I showered her with the details of two-hour feedings—which required pumping my milk until my breasts hurt, adding special protein and carbohydrates to the milk, and feeding him about two tablespoons at a time—measuring minuscule amounts of heart medications, remeasuring even more minuscule amounts of medication after he threw up the first dose . . .

As I continued the exacting details of my days, her eyes took on a glazed, frozen expression. That told me all I needed to know—she didn't want to hear all this.

"Oh," she said, looking desperately around. "I'm glad he's doing better." She quickly took herself as far across the room as possible.

"Better?" I thought incredulously.

Someone tapped me on the shoulder, and turning I got a quick hug from another friend. She asked, "How's he doing?"

"Well, I was up at midnight, 2 A.M., again at 4 . . ." I launched right in again. But before I had even completed two more sentences, she too wore that glazed, overwhelmed expression. I stopped mid-sentence, took a deep breath, and said, "We're all still adjusting. Thanks for asking."

I realized in those two encounters that I had a choice in responding to people's questions. In the future I needed to determine whom to "educate" about our situation and whom to give brief answers to. I just needed to develop a wise heart to discern between the two.

It takes time and painful encounters to learn how much to say to whom. It takes a heart that has been tuned to God's wisdom. How? By praying specifically for discernment. Remember that James said, "Be . . . slow to speak." It means drawing in a deep enough breath to direct a prayer heavenward for God to fill your mouth with the right words—words of truth, not hurt and anger. "For man's anger does not bring about the righteous life that God desires" (James 1:20).

We have a tremendous responsibility to honor the Lord in the way we represent Him while communicating about our child's condition. Not that we can't fail or be truthful in how awful and difficult life can be, but ultimately we must reflect God's faithfulness. If for no other reason, we honor the Lord for the sake of our very own chronic child!

In Colossians Paul prays for a wise heart to be able to represent Christ clearly and effectively. Our prayer can parallel his. "Pray that I may proclaim it clearly, as I should. Be wise in the way you act toward outsiders; make the most of every opportunity. Let your conversation be always full of grace, seasoned with salt, so that you may know how to answer everyone" (4:4-6). Wow! This is a pretty clear guideline for becoming effective communicators for Christ. Look at each of the elements of these verses:

1) *First pray.* You can't be tuned in to how or what the Lord wants you to say if you haven't opened your lines of connection with Him.

2) *Proclaim clearly.* This is again where story comes into play. Relating your story, even practicing it to immunize yourself to the sharpness of the words, helps you to be clear in your communication. To tell your story concisely, relate it in chronological order, and always bring your listener back to God's divine hand in your child's life.

3) *Be wise in the way you act.* Wise, not just in the words you say, but in the way you say them. Your story may be clear, but what is your body language saying? When you talk about your child and condition, do you cross your arms across your chest—sending the message of "back off?" Your actions can discredit even the most practiced story or comments.

4) *Make the most of every opportunity.* Do you notice little cracks in conversations, little opportunities to share about your child and his life? Do you step forward in confidence to tell of God's faithfulness in your family's life, or do you shrink back with timidity? "For God did not give us a spirit of timidity, but a spirit of power" (2 Timothy 1:7). Taking these opportunities to plant seeds of hope in other people's hearts may be part of the purpose of your child's condition.

5) *Conversations full of grace.* What's grace in this context? It's a tenderness. It's a dying-to-self response so that another can be edified.

It's not striking out with words of hurt, anger, or bitterness. In conversations grace is saying healing words, offering a balm of kindness.

6) *Seasoned with salt.* Salt is a temporary agitator, with the potential to aid healing. Another way this could have been said is "sprinkled with salt." The need for salt in conversation is to bring a little correction into what you say. Perhaps a word of instruction or education is necessary for the person you're talking to. Maybe he has unintentionally said something hurtful. You have an opportunity to offer a dash of salt by redirecting what he has said. If you gently correct him (with grace!), he will know how to respond to similar situations in the future. You've done him a great service.

Paul's instruction is a tall order, something we can strive for. Don't feel guilty if you can't yet measure up to this nearly perfect, timely way of responding. As with everything, it will take time to develop responses that instruct, are tactful, and full of grace.

Your child's condition is your unique calling and avenue to minister to others. You may not feel qualified or ready now in these early stages and years of adjustment. Don't feel pressured to "arrive" just yet. It's through the process over the next several years that your story will take on a profound quality with a heavenly impact. Just know now that with each encounter with friends and acquaintances, you are adding another layer of understanding for your friends. Your patience with unwitting friends extends the same grace Christ modeled for us. As parents of a chronic child, we have a challenge for ministry toward which we can strive and pray. We can use our situation to comfort and bring hope to others.

The Spirit of the Sovereign LORD is on me, because the LORD has anointed me to preach good news to the poor. He has sent me to bind up the brokenhearted, to proclaim freedom for the captives and release from darkness for the prisoners, to proclaim the year of the LORD's favor and the day of vengeance of our God, to comfort all who mourn, and provide for those who grieve in Zion—to bestow on them a crown of beauty instead of ashes, the oil of gladness instead of mourning, and a garment of praise instead of a spirit of despair. They will be called oaks of righteousness, a planting of the LORD for the display of his splendor. (Isaiah 61:1)

PRACTICAL MATTERS

Develop words and phrases you can use to waylay the hard questions or comments from others. Use these as a protective shield until you discern if the person you're speaking to is safe for you emotionally.

Pray about how your story and your child's story can be used. Once you're at a point where you feel ready to share what's gone on in your family's life, ask the Lord to put people in your path who need to hear your words. Remember, it's hope you want to offer, always directing people to the Lord through your story.

Suggested Reading

Differences in Common by Marilyn Trainer (not faith-based)

10

MARY

When visiting the beach during the summer months, sometimes I cringe when Robbie takes his shirt off. I have to brace myself for the inevitable stares and piteous looks people give him when they see his scar. It runs from the base of his throat to his navel, a knit line that has grown with him as he's grown taller.

It's only been as he's reached preadolescence that he's become self-conscious about it. To the inevitable questions other children ask, and for Robbie's benefit, I explain it this way: "Robbie is a soldier in the army of the Lord. He is proof of God's divine plan. That scar is a battle scar that he wears proudly and with honor."

"MOMMY, WHY?" AND OTHER HARD QUESTIONS

The Lord will fulfill his purpose for me; your love, O Lord,
endures forever—do not abandon the works of your hands.

PSALM 138:8

As parents and caretakers we assume responsibility for our children's care—as we should until they are old enough to care for themselves. But in shouldering that responsibility, sometimes we overlook how our children perceive themselves and the condition of their bodies. We need to remember this is *his* life, *his* body, *his* disease. Does your child see the condition as a part of who he is, or as a separate problem that Mom and Dad take care of?

The answer to that depends partly on the condition. For children born into a chronic illness, that's all they know. From their early memories life has been like this for them. They may not have as many questions. If there was no "before" for their condition, they don't struggle with the implications of "after."

On the other hand, children who acquire their condition, especially after the age of clear memory, may plague you with many questions. They'll ask you about God. They'll ask you about dying. They'll ask you about their future. They'll ask how long their condition is going to last. They'll ask why it doesn't go away.

Children who require constant hands-on medical care from Mom and Dad may see the disease as somewhat separate from themselves. The illness, disease, or condition is something that has happened *to* them. It's necessary for Mom and Dad to perform a task *for* them. Conditions such as epilepsy, environmental allergies, diabetes, asthma, food allergies, cystic fibrosis, and so on are more invasive. These require doing something to the child's body.

ELIZABETH

While Jordan was still in the hospital, just a few days after diagnosis, he fought with me about receiving his shot. The nurses had administered his injections up to that point, but now it was time for me to take over. As he kicked at me, he screamed, "I want to go home. I want to go home!"

I sensed there was more to what he was saying than what was on the surface. I asked him, "What's at home?"

He sobbed, "I want to go home and leave diabetes here in the bed!"

I knew the permanence of his disease was nearly beyond his cognitive ability to understand. I said gently, "Jordan, diabetes is part of you now. It will be with you wherever you go, here and at home."

He continued to cry, and the nurse helped me hold him down for his shot. I kept my composure until I was done with him and then began to cry too. If I couldn't fathom the finality of the disease, how could I possibly explain it well enough to my son so he could accept it?

When children see the condition as separate from themselves, they'll have a harder time reconciling it with the rest of their lives. They'll consider it an intrusion and treat it with animosity. Your goal is to help them not only accept the condition, but recognize how it adds to and actually complements their lives. As an analogy, consider three-dimensional vision as opposed to screen vision. Three-D has depth and contours and shades; screen vision is flat and void of texture. Your child's condition adds depth to his or her life; it's multifaceted.

Your child is in a process of becoming—becoming what, we don't know. But God does. We can instill faith and hope in our children that there will be depth to their testimony, that their lives will unfold in 3-D. God promises all His children, grown and young, that once we are part of His family, He has a plan for our story. Second Corinthians

1:21-22 confirms this with a promise: "He anointed us, set his seal of ownership on us, and put his Spirit in our hearts as a deposit, guaranteeing what is to come." Guaranteeing what? Promising a future in Him because we belong to Him. From Jesus' own mouth we learn that we belong to Him and have a future. "The sheep listen to his voice. He calls his own sheep by name and leads them out" (John 10:3).

Your job is to help your child grow into that secure place of *knowing* that her condition has a divine purpose. You can't answer your child's questions why until you are reasonably secure in the answers yourself. Go back and reread chapter 3 if you continue to struggle with the same questions your child asks. The conclusion we drew there was that through your child's condition God will be glorified. "Let us hold unswervingly to the hope we profess, for he who promised is faithful" (Hebrews 10:23). Unswerving. Straight-arrowed in God's path, knowing that our hope and the fulfillment of God's promises lie along His route.

PREVENTING GUILT

Some children with chronic illness may feel responsible for bringing their condition into the family. They may say, "It's my fault," or you may recognize signs of guilt—self-blame, degrading comments about themselves, apologizing for things when they don't need to. Even the very words of childhood songs may seem hollow and empty of promise. "Jesus loves me? It sure doesn't feel like He does!"

Allow them to express their full feelings, but then redirect them to the truths you have learned about their condition. The child did not make it happen, nor was there anything she did to cause it to happen. She isn't being punished. She isn't to blame.

Your child's freedom from self-blame lies in her confidence in her personhood in Christ. The Lord loves her (and therefore she can sing, "Jesus loves me") because He loves what He created—differences and all.

A year after Melanie was diagnosed with severe asthma, she drew a picture that gave me reassurance that she didn't feel guilty and had accepted Christ's love for her. The picture was of a simple brown cross with a stick figure on it. The words from the cross were, "You

*are a good girl. I love you." The other little figure next to the cross
said simply, "I love you too." My heart was so blessed to see that
what we had spoken to Melanie about Christ's love for her had
become a reality to her.*

                              Cliff—dad to nine-year-old Melanie

Your child may not be of an age to be able to fully internalize the
truths of Scripture promises, but that shouldn't stop you from repeating words, Scripture, and songs to him. It's never too early or too late
for him to hear God's Word. Even if he can't fully comprehend its
implications, you are helping to hide it in his heart (Psalm 19:11).
There it will be available for him to feed on as he grows older. The
impact of God's Word won't diminish over time. These verses will
become so imbedded in his heart that they will float into his conscience right at his point of need when he is a young adult. God is
faithful to use His Word in this way. "Let the word of Christ dwell in
you richly as you teach and admonish one another with all wisdom,
and as you sing psalms, hymns and spiritual songs with gratitude in
your hearts to God" (Colossians 3:16).

NONVERBAL QUESTIONS

Your child may not be old enough to express questions verbally. You
know him or her better than anyone else, but you can still learn more.
Pray for discernment of subtle signs that will tell you what is going
on in his or her mind.

It will take a discerning ear and heart to understand what your
child is communicating nonverbally. Does she get angry right before
medication time? Does he knock your Bible out of your hands at family devotion time? Does he cover your mouth when you're talking on
the phone with his nurse or doctor? Does she stomp to her room and
slam the door when you try to talk with her about her condition?

What is your child saying? *I don't like this. I'm mad at God. Stop talking about me. I don't want to deal with this!* How do you respond to these
nonverbal concerns? First ask him if what you've discerned is what
he's really feeling. Probe for the reason for his actions. Give his action
a name. Don't put words in his mouth, but ask, "Every time we read

the Bible, you knock it out of my hands. Are you mad?" He might yell and scream and admit to his anger. Or he might catch you off guard and say, "No, I'm not mad. I just don't understand the words in that Bible. I want to use mine!" Once you've figured out the issue, then you can begin to address it in a way he can understand.

Give your child appropriate and safe ways to express herself. She needs to know it's okay to feel angry, unhappy, or even express a need to be out of control for a time. If you prevent or punish her for the way she works out her issues, you haven't truly allowed her to work through them. Think of acceptable ways she can express herself. Let her finger-paint on a huge piece of paper on the kitchen floor. Buy her a punching bag and gloves and let her duke it out with the bag. Older kids can have a private drawing book or journal to scribble in or draw what they are feeling. Invest in a basketball and hoop. Physical exercise helps to vent and redirect anger. Show them how to use this method of release, and then give them permission to express what they want within clear, safe boundaries that you have established (i.e., no punching people or no painting the walls).

It takes a lot of parenting wisdom and even trial and error to piece together the formula that will allow your child to express himself or herself. Your wisdom in addressing your child's questions and actions will build up your entire family. Proverbs offers multiple promises for people seeking wisdom. This God-given wisdom will provide you with the right responses at the right time, with the right words for your child. "By wisdom a house is built, and through understanding it is established; through knowledge its rooms are filled with rare and beautiful treasures" (Proverbs 24:3-4). You have the authority and power, through gaining spiritual wisdom and understanding, to lay a solid foundation and "build" your house—your home, your family. With knowledge of your child and his or her specific needs, you will fill your home with eternal, heavenly treasures. That's worth praying for!

VERBAL QUESTIONS

Older children can articulate specific questions, and the deeper query behind these may send you staggering. You suddenly realize you aren't the only one dealing with the hows and whys! The questions are loaded with issues of faith, trust, and insecurity.

If it's appropriate, have your child read chapter 3 of this book, or read it with her. Explain the Scripture references and memorize them as a family.

You need to be truthful in your answers to their questions. Children are perceptive. They'll know if you're hiding the truth, lying, or dismissing their questions. You can say that you're not sure of the answer if you don't know. Or you can respond by saying you need to look something up. You can even say you need to ask your doctor for an answer. Use your pastor as a resource for spiritual questions. Your role is to make sure children know you are approachable and will try to find the answers for them if you can't provide them yourself. Your child needs to know you can be trusted with their concerns and are committed to following through to answer their questions.

Perhaps you read these words and think, *But I don't feel qualified!* You know what *does* qualify you to be the best teacher for your child? Simply that God chose you to parent this child. You may still be in the process of developing the skills to answer his or her questions; God doesn't expect you to know all the answers. But He is equipping you even while you are still short on answers. In 2 Corinthians 12:9, Paul quotes Christ, offering this assurance of qualification: "My grace is sufficient for you, for my power is made perfect in weakness."

Try praying this prayer: "May God himself, the God of peace, sanctify [me] through and through" (1 Thessalonians 5:23). Sanctify you completely. Sanctified means set apart or prepared. This prayer will help prepare you to meet the challenges now and ahead. God has also anointed you to parent your chronic child. Being anointed means equipped by God Himself for a task He has entrusted to you. Why did He entrust it to *you*? Because there is nobody better to do the job.

TALKING ABOUT DEATH

A trite answer to questions about death will only erode the trust you're building between you and your children. A general, dismissive promise that they are going to be "fine" is not an answer. As painful and scary as it is to talk about the possibility of dying and death, you must talk about it in detail.

A good place to start is to find out what they want to know. Do they wonder what heaven is like? Are they unclear about what they have to do to be sure they will go there?

This is a great opportunity to talk with them about their salvation. If they accepted Christ as small children, remind them of that experience. If they want to renew their commitment to Christ, encourage them to do so. It's important that they confess their sins in this process too. Even though they seem innocent as children, they must be reminded of their need for a Savior. The free gift of salvation is dependent on recognizing they cannot go to heaven simply by being "good." There is a basic promise any child can understand, even a child with extreme limitations: "Jesus loves me."

We've talked about raising children to be "whole." Regardless of their outer or inner physical condition, they were created with whole spirits. Though their bodies may be broken, their spirits are intact. That whole spirit is capable of accepting the ministering touch of Christ. The medical field may not know how much children with brain damage can comprehend. But as Christians we do know Christ is capable of touching them in a way and in a place in their spirits that medical science can't understand.

Jesus reminded the disciples to allow children to seek Him and draw near to Him. "But Jesus called the children to him and said, 'Let the little children come to me, and do not hinder them, for the kingdom of heaven belongs to such as these'" (Matthew 19:14). We certainly don't want to "hinder" children with incomplete information, nor do we want to assume they can't fathom the implications of Jesus' love. In all circumstances, even as grim as they may seem, we need to help our children to know that Christ is approachable, loving, and involved in their lives.

"MOMMY, I WANT TO DIE."

It may seem to your child, particularly if she is in pain, that being with Jesus would "feel" a whole lot more comfortable. While, yes, it's true she would no longer feel the discomforts of her disease after she dies, you have a responsibility to be sure that your child doesn't think of taking her life as a way to end her suffering.

ELIZABETH

> *When Jordan objects to getting shots, sometimes I have to remind him, and even occasionally not very gently, of the absolute necessity for insulin. Without it he would die. Sometimes he responds as a typical angry nine-year-old might: "I don't care!" Then I tell him exactly what death would mean.*
>
> *Death would mean being separated from his family. As much as I'd like to leave it there with a scare tactic to shake him up a bit, I need to go on to explain where he will go if he dies. He has accepted Christ as his Savior, and he knows he's going to heaven, so the thought of being with Jesus is good. But as his parents, we don't know what the consequence of a person taking his or her own life might be. We have had to remind him that God's perfect plan is to wait for His timing.*
>
> *I cannot allow Jordan to think that making a choice that would lead to his death would be the way Jesus would want to see him arrive in heaven. I must convey to Jordan the necessity of living out the life that God has given him. We are not in a position to challenge or alter God's plan.*

If your child repeatedly talks about wanting to die, particularly an older child who would have the means to end his or her life, *take it seriously*. This is a sign of depression, which can lead to suicide. Clinical depression, especially in the chronically ill, is extremely dangerous. Thought patterns are warped, and common sense may be nonexistent. They may think that the *only* escape is through death. To them there is no hope. Death becomes an obsessive thought, dominating their words and actions.

Even if you're not sure that your child is clinically depressed, but he or she does talk about death frequently, seek professional help. Be especially alert to young adults and teenagers, who truly may not be able to bear the thought of their condition continuing for the rest of their lives, particularly if they have just been diagnosed. Hormones cause some teens to feel out of control much of the time anyway. They may need help from professionals to deal with their emotions and the implications of the condition and to apply their faith.

FACING YOUR FEAR OF LOSING YOUR CHILD

It's a tough lesson to embrace that our children are ours for but a short time. Whether one dies at a young age or moves out of the house at an older age, we are constantly in the process of giving them up, relinquishing them back to the Lord.

A parent has a unique bond with a chronic child. You are intimately involved in every part of his or her life. You can read this child better, you understand his or her thoughts, you know every nuance of every action. You have a deeper connection with him or her because the chronic condition requires it.

If your chronic child died, her very being would be ripped from your heart, leaving a painful wound that would never completely heal. No wonder we cling to our chronic kids just a little tighter. No wonder we rock them in our laps long past the time they fit comfortably there. Your child's life is more precious to you because you know how tenuous it is. All chronic conditions have a perilous side. All have a sense of a constant menace, threatening to snatch your child if you turn your back.

That's our human response. But Jesus said, "I give them eternal life, and they shall never perish; no one can snatch them out of my hand. My Father, who has given them to me, is greater than all; no one can snatch them out of my Father's hand" (John 10:28-29). In other words, your child cannot face an "untimely" death when he or she is a child of the Lord. Death can't "snatch" this child because he or she is securely nestled in the palm of God's hand. As your child's parents, God has His hand extended to you for you to nurture and parent your child while in His protection. When a child dies, he or she hasn't left His hand. The child is still there. God has just drawn His hand away from you and closer to His heart.

Our reassurance lies in this: "Since the children have flesh and blood, he too shared in their humanity so that by his death he might destroy him who holds the power of death" (Hebrews 2:14). Christ took away the finality of permanent death when He died and rose again. The child of God will not be separated from Him. Christ's death ensures that your child will stay firmly in His grip. "See, I have engraved you on the palms of my hands" (Isaiah 49:16). Read this verse to your child, substituting his or her name for the word *you*. It becomes very personal, doesn't it?

HIS FINISHED WORK

Of course we can't say for certain your child is not going to die soon. He or she could very well be struck by a car and die tomorrow or have a fatal complication of his condition. This is a hard concept to accept, but the timing of your child's death has already been predetermined by God. We can't change that fact. "All the days ordained for me were written in your book before one of them came to be" (Psalms 139:16).

The assurance we can have as parents is that our children will not die until Christ has finished his work *in* them and His work *through* them. We don't know when God will be "done," when the mission for your child's life will be over, but we can know that in its completion God will be glorified and honored. For that reason we believe that it doesn't seem *likely* that your child will die soon, because there are so many opportunities your child and family will have to "show off" God! But even after death, your child's story will have an impact. Our story doesn't end with death.

This is the rock-solid foundation for raising whole kids. When they die, having accepted Christ, they will become whole in body once again. They are always whole in spirit, but in death they'll have a new body, free of disease and limitations. "So will it be with the resurrection of the dead. The body that is sown is perishable, it is raised imperishable; it is sown in dishonor, it is raised in glory; it is sown in weakness, it is raised in power; it is sown a natural body, it is raised a spiritual body" (1 Corinthians 15:42-44).

How can you communicate these truths to your children? If they are of an age of accountability, talk with them about accepting Christ as their Savior and what that means. If they aren't old enough or have limited cognitive ability, simply saturate them with God's Word by reading Scripture to them and playing Christian music. God's Spirit will minister to them in a way and via an avenue that they can understand. "The Lord is not slow in keeping his promise. . . . He is patient with you, not wanting anyone to perish" (2 Peter 3:9).

God *always* has an avenue to communicate with your child. Your responsibility is to expose your child to God's Word. The Lord promises: "So is my word that goes out from my mouth: It will not return empty, but will accomplish what I desire and achieve the purpose for which I sent it" (Isaiah 55:11). The Word of God never goes out uselessly. Praying God's divine truth over your child who cannot make a personal verbal decision brings you peace. You know that His Word is being embedded in your child's soul.

There's another profound promise for families in Isaiah. It's a "generational" promise we can claim that gives us confidence for our children's future. As faithful parents when we impart the Word of God to our children, God will be faithful to guard it in them. "'As for me, this is my covenant with them,' says the Lord. 'My Spirit, who is on you, and my words that I have put in your mouth will not depart from your mouth, or from the mouths of your children, or from the mouths of their descendants from this time on and forever,' says the Lord" (Isaiah 59:21).

PRACTICAL MATTERS

Ask your children to draw pictures or write a poem about their condition. Encourage younger children to draw a picture of themselves with Jesus. You can also draw a picture to show them how you view *your* relationship with Him. Pick several verses that you can illustrate with your children, perhaps verses from the Psalms that talk about nature.

Suggested Reading

    Heaven: Your Real Home by Joni Eareckson Tada
    Young People and Chronic Illness by Kelly Huegel (not faith-based)

11

It seems we're in and out of the hospital all winter. Flu bugs, viruses, and even "common" colds send Caitlyn dangerously close to pneumonia. I know lots of people pray for us, but I feel completely ineffective in my prayers. Sometimes I just want to curl up in a ball and pull the covers over my head. Shouldn't I be the strongest prayer warrior for my child?

When she gets so sick she has to be hospitalized, all I want to do is scoop her out of the bed and rush back home, back to our nest of safety. But if I run away every time she gets sick or every time I'm scared about her future, what does that say to her? What am I teaching her if on the heels of every adverse situation I run for the sanctuary of home?

Lois—mother of twelve-year-old Caitlyn with cystic fibrosis

AWAY FROM HOME

*My people will live in peaceful dwelling places, in secure homes,
in undisturbed places of rest.*

ISAIAH 32:18

What do you most look forward to after a trip to the doctor's? At
the end of a long day at work? Or after shopping? Or at the end of
a vacation?

Going home.

Home is the place we all retreat to; it is a safe haven of rest where
we can be who we are without the need to keep up an appearance. We
can be ourselves, without make-up or hair combed, sans shower, and
teeth unbrushed because we are accepted for who we are.

Home is a safe harbor, a quiet port in the midst of stormy seas, a
place of order in a world of crashing chaos.

For children with a chronic condition, home is like a sheltered
greenhouse, protecting them from outside adverse forces. Like a new
little seedling, your chronic kid is still unfolding his new form and
pushing down tender roots, finding courage to face ongoing challenges. Gradually, as he gains strength, his roots toughen, and he
becomes better able to deal with the cold winds that wait outside the
greenhouse. Trusting God becomes the root system for this fragile
flower. And once God establishes those roots, nothing is going to hinder this child's growth!

Initially, part of our job as parents is to nurture, build, and pre-
serve our children's sense of worth, which is easy to do in the home
environment. We can readily build positive experiences into everyday

home life. We can actively avoid situations in which our children are devalued.

But are we meant to be isolationists forever, never interacting with others? "Overprotection may appear on the surface to be kind, but it can really be evil. An oversupply can smother people emotionally, squeeze the life out of their hopes and expectations, and strip them of dignity."[5]

Look back at the verse that heads this chapter and think about the meaning of Isaiah 32:18, which claims peace and rest where we dwell. Isaiah is pointing us to Christ; after all, we are His people. Now read Romans 8:21: "If God is for us, who can be against us?" There are parallel points in these two verses: Jesus will always be with us, and if He is always with us, who can possibly stand against us? He is the reason that we have peace, and He is not relegated to just our homes. He travels wherever we go, bringing us promised peace in every situation. "You will keep in perfect peace him whose mind is steadfast, because he trusts in you" (Isaiah 26:3).

Sometimes we actually have to take a deep breath before stepping out into the storm, but try to visualize Christ leading you, going before you and beckoning to you to follow Him wherever He leads. Do you trust Him enough to go with Him? Will you trust Him as you step out of the sunny greenhouse and get ready for the challenges that face your family away from home?

FACING CHALLENGES

It takes courage to interact with the world head-on when you have a child with a chronic condition. Our fears that our child will be stared at, pointed to, or singled out may blind us to the rich experiences and challenges she *must* face in order to live a full life without stagnating fear.

Courage comes in many different guises. Courage is the ability to persevere even in the face of fear; it is the desire to be independent; it is the strength to get out of bed in the morning and walk through the day, knowing that every moment is an act of extreme determination.

For your child it may be as simple as riding the school bus by herself, walking down the driveway to get the mail, or answering the phone when it rings. Maybe it's the act of getting herself dressed for the first time or the initial act of taking control of her special diet.

> *Jessie refused to think that her blindness made her different from other kids. One morning she overheard Dick and me talking about who would be taking her to Sunday school, and she interrupted us to say, "I want to go by myself." I was dumbfounded, not knowing what to say. How on earth was she going to find her way by herself? I stammered, trying to find a good excuse for not letting her do it, when she lifted her little chin defiantly and said, "If you'll string a rope from the end of the parking lot to the front door of the church, I can find my way from there to my classroom by myself." So that's exactly what we did. Her determination and grit humbled me. I saw only the obstacles; she already had the solution.*
>
> Margaret—*mother of seven-year-old Jessie*

Allowing your child to take such safe risks will begin to turn any "disability" into "this ability." Maybe he can't ride a bicycle, but he does have the ability to ride a three-wheeler. Maybe he can't say "aluminum foil," but he has the ability to answer the phone, speaking slowly and politely.

Teaching your child personal dignity becomes the first set of delicate new leaves as he grows toward personal independence. Remind him of his special uniqueness to God. Help him memorize Psalm 139:14-16, which points out God's loving, perfect sovereignty *in the specific instance of your child's creation:* "For you created my inmost being; you knit me together in my mother's womb. I praise you because I am fearfully and wonderfully made; your works are wonderful, I know that full well. My frame was not hidden from you when I was made in the secret place. When I was woven together in the depths of the earth, your eyes saw my unformed body. All the days ordained for me were written in your book before one of them came to be."

Each of us was created by God's hand with all genetic components already keyed in. God allowed even those conditions that happened as a result of an accident or other outside forces. Embracing this special uniqueness becomes the second pair of new leaves unfurled in your child's quest for personal independence.

Eventually, the time comes to send your little sprout into situations outside your controlled home environment. You see in her a maturity, an ability to handle herself and her disease in a new way. Test her growing confidence with safe challenges. Even in failure, determination can take root. Does she feel safe enough to take the risk again, or will she shy away the next time for fear of failing?

Our children learn from what they see mirrored in our reactions to their successes or failures. Our reactions are like water and fertilizer to a plant. Our encouragement feeds them, but if we withhold support and trust, they shrivel quickly.

Have you ever tried taking no out of your vocabulary for one day? It's startling how often we stymie our children's desire for independence because of our own issues of fear, frustration, or plain laziness. Admit it—isn't it easier to say no than to agree to something that's going to take up some of your time and energy? But if instead we say yes and then support them (to whatever degree needed), we allow our children the chance to mature and possibly gain mastery over an area they think of as a challenge.

DEVELOPING COURAGE

Courage makes us think of the Cowardly Lion from the *Wizard of Oz*. Remember him singing in his rough, childlike voice, "If I were king of the forest"? That is a song of "if onlys," if ever there was one! The Cowardly Lion failed to recognize the ability for courageous acts buried deep within *himself*. He had just never had anyone believe in him enough for him to believe in himself.

MARY

> *Robbie wanted in the worst way to play baseball. My heart sank. I worried about him not being able to keep up with the other kids; his coordination was somewhat delayed. But I couldn't think of a valid reason to say no. It seemed a safe risk.*

He lagged behind his teammates for most of the season—never getting a hit when up at bat. When he was at home, he'd spend hours practicing hitting grounders and pop-up flies. Dana and I talked about pulling him off the team. I wanted to take him and run far, far away to some safe, distant place. Dana realized that if we took him off the team, Robbie might think we didn't have faith in his own determination. He was afraid Robbie wouldn't have the courage to try again at something else.

Finally it was the last game of the season. Our team was losing. It was the last inning and Rob's last chance up at bat (you know, the whole horrible scenario you've seen a hundred times on TV and in movies). I was praying forcefully, clenching my teeth, sweat greasing my palms, when suddenly Robbie caught the ball off the end of his bat and plugged it neatly up the middle between first and second base.

He momentarily froze, then let out a shout and ran like the dickens for first base. Then he burst into tears as he was called out. Everyone tried to comfort him, thinking he was disappointed because he'd been called out. I knew in my heart that wasn't the reason for his tears. He was crying for joy, ecstatic over his hit.

I hugged him when he ran up to the bench. "Mom," he said, "I remembered to pray before I got up to bat that time. That's what made the difference!" His face shone with delight. It didn't matter to him that he'd been called out. He had faced a challenge and won.

Oh, and by the way, even though Rob was out, his pop fly brought someone home, and they won their division championship!

What courage! Our children's zest for challenges will humble us, stopping us dead in our tracks, and making us realize that there is a person of grit, zest, triumph, and zeal developing behind those enormous brown eyes and tousled blond hair.

PHYSICAL CHALLENGES

Does your child's condition mean he has a physical difference that makes him stand out in a crowd? Is he in a wheelchair? Does she use crutches or a cane? Does she have scars, tubes, a hearing aid? Some differences are obvious; others are more subtle. A child may feel he looks physically different even if others don't perceive it. On the other hand, some children don't think they look any different, and yet others around them see something obvious.

People, especially children, react to things they perceive as "unusual" or "special." A young child will cling to a parent's hand and try to hide if he or she hasn't had positive experiences with someone who looks or acts different. Occasionally an adult will be the one to pull a child away, perhaps fearing that the difference is contagious, and her child will "catch it." It's hard not to bare your teeth and snarl when others stare or make comments or whisper behind a hand.

Rabid Mother vs. Mother Tiger

MARY

> *We were on a routine trip to the grocery store. In the cookie aisle Robbie asked if we could buy some chocolate chip cookies, but he said, "Chawquit chip." I knew what he meant. A little boy and his mother were passing by, and the little boy pointed at Robbie, giggled, and said loudly, "He doesn't know how to say it right; he talks funny!"*
>
> *Robbie's lower lip started to tremble, and he looked up at me with tear-filled eyes. "Mommy, why did tha' boy lauff a' me?"*
>
> *I snarled in a voice loud enough to carry for several city blocks: "Because that little boy's mother has never taught him MANNERS!"*

The rabid mother snarls and snaps at anyone who approaches her cub, regardless of their intentions. She reacts viscerally when strangers stare—wanting to tear at their prying eyes. Claws out, teeth bared, she approaches the world defensively, spewing bitter words on anyone within hearing.

At a school play I was busy signing to BJ, unaware of a little girl who came and stood at my elbow watching everything I did. BJ signed to me that she was there. She tapped me on the shoulder and asked, "What are you doing? How come he doesn't talk?"

My gut contracted at first, but I took a deep breath and explained that BJ was deaf, and this was the way we talked to each other. Then I said, "BJ is about your age. Have you lost your first tooth yet? BJ just lost his today!" She ended up dragging her whole family over to meet us and pleaded with her mother to let me teach her sign language so she could talk with her new friend BJ.

Debbie—mother of six-year-old BJ

The mother tiger, on the other hand, is one who uses opportunities as a chance to teach. If you plan on being out and about in your community and your child's disability is visible, your family has the unique chance to influence the attitudes of others. The mother tiger protects her young from unkindness, ridicule, and pain, but she allows the cub to venture from the den and experience life on his own.

SALT AND LIGHT

"You are the light of the world. A city on a hill cannot be hidden" (Matthew 5:13). Our Christian influence is meant to be salt and light to the world. We are to be seen, even in all our messiness and unpleasantness, so the world can see God's grace and glory working in our lives. If we stay hidden in our homes, away from the prying public eye, what are we saying about our belief in God's sovereignty, His plan, His perfect will for our child?

God always gives good gifts to His children. His good gifts to your family are probably readily apparent to you; now make it apparent to others. Pray for opportunities with your children to be a messenger, an ambassador, salt and light to the world.

PRACTICAL MATTERS

Occasional hospitalizations are a fact of life for children with chronic conditions. Most children will have fears and questions about being in the hospital. Consider these ideas as you prepare for such a time:

Give your child a sense of control by allowing him or her to choose things such as foods to eat, what to wear, what to pack, which arm to have the IV in, what to watch on TV, etc.

Research childhood development and find out what would be an appropriate response to hospitalization for your child's age. For example: Babies want comfort through touch and holding; between six months and three years a child will experience extreme separation anxiety and be very clingy; four-to-six-year-olds have fears about "losing" something from their body; six-to-twelve-year-olds fear abandonment and change of body image; teens deal with feelings of loss, may feel out-of-control, or have an altered body image.

When at all possible, stay with your child in the hospital or alternate staying with your spouse. Through your church and friends, arrange for prayer coverage for the entire stay in the hospital.

12

I would get so frustrated at my son's inability to process things quickly. I worried about his future, who he would become. Though he was only in first grade, he always seemed to be behind, not quite picking up what he needed to learn. I didn't know if it was because of his hearing impairment or if he had a learning disability.

But then I realized he was always the first one to help me when chores needed to be done—dishes washed, floors vacuumed. He was cheerful, and he didn't seem to get frustrated by his lack of academic savvy. He had a contented disposition and a happy countenance. When I recognized this, my heart swelled with love. All of a sudden, the other things didn't seem to matter as much.

Debbie—mother of six-year-old BJ

EDUCATIONAL CHOICES

And Jesus grew in wisdom and stature, and in favor
with God and men.

LUKE 2:52

Picture this scene: A hot, dusty road filled with lowing camels, braying donkeys, and people shuffling along in the brassy late afternoon sun on the trail from Jerusalem after the Feast of the Passover. Just as the campsite is reached and tents are erected, a young mother suddenly realizes her twelve-year-old son is not among the hundred or so relatives and friends who are traveling together. She and her husband quickly become frantic, searching everywhere until, with haste, they retrace their route back to Jerusalem. After three days they find Him in the temple courts, "sitting among the teachers, listening to them and asking them questions. Everyone who heard him was amazed at his understanding and his answers" (Luke 2:46-47).

The child is, of course, Jesus. He responds to his parents' astonished questions with a question of his own: "Why were you searching for me? . . . Didn't you know I had to be in my Father's house?" (v. 49). In the King James Version the end of the verse reads: "I must be about my Father's business," as if it were the most natural thing in the world for him to disappear for three days to be in the house of the Lord, preparing at the tender age of twelve for his life ministry. His parents must have felt bewilderment! Even though Mary and Joseph recognized to some extent what Jesus' life work would be, they did not understand how he was to prepare for it. His pursuit of education was being orchestrated by a higher hand than those of his earthly parents. It was God's plan for His Son that prompted Jesus to leave his family and seek out the wise council of the men in the synagogue in Jerusalem.

How can we apply this to our children? Our heart's desire for the education of each of our children should be that we would teach them how to effectively be about our Father's business and that they would have a deep desire to seek out God's way for their lives.

THE PURSUIT OF EXCELLENCE

The purpose of education is to equip children to fulfill God's calling on their lives. The development of a Christlike character, a growing faith, and academic excellence are the foundational posts on which we build our educational structure. Every family, regardless of the type of chronic condition you face with your child, should create a plan for education. Even the severely disabled child benefits from setting goals to prevent aimless drifting through life. Without goals these children are in danger of becoming burdens to their parents and, as they mature, to society as well. Everyone can contribute something. Also personal accomplishment is a source of confidence in one's ability, which is better than shame in one's disability.

"People were meant to complement each other. Where I am strong, you may be weak. At points where you excel, I may be all thumbs. And the ultimate tragedy comes when I reject you because of your (differences), and you reject me because of mine. Then we live apart . . . and we die apart. We will die without ever really knowing each other or experiencing the rich contributions each could have made in the other's life."[6]

People of all types become richer for their interactions with others. As children relate with those who have differences, the "difference" quickly disappears from the equation. Later in life when they become doctors, lawyers, teachers, policemen, etc., they are at ease, comfortable working with someone with a chronic condition.

But who is responsible for the education of our children? The government? Society? The church? Ourselves?

OUR HERITAGE

While we were writing this chapter, the nation was shocked by the senseless violence in a Colorado community when two teenage boys walked into Columbine High School and massacred twelve students and one teacher, wounded sixteen others, and then turned the guns on themselves. Stunned families learned of the tragic events as the media displayed scenes of the small town of Littleton locked in mourning. Police experts discovered bomb-making equipment in plain view at the boys' homes, and they found diaries that detailed their plan of destruction. Questions were raised: Who was responsible? The teens? What responsibility should the parents have for the actions of their children?

God's plan for the family is for parents to have the ultimate authority over their children. "Sons are a heritage from the Lord, children a reward from him" (Psalm 127:3). He entrusts specific children to particular parents with the understanding that those parents will uphold their stewardship responsibilities.

> *God has set children under their parents' control for approximately one-third of their lives. Unlike animals that raise their young for only a few months, children are dependent on their parents for an extensive training period. Animals need to receive training for physical existence, but a child requires training for his soul. Parents are responsible to train their children according to God's standards. It is, therefore, the primary duty of parents to guide their children's lives for the purposes of God, and to train them as He would have them trained.*[7]

CHALLENGING CHOICES

What motivates you when you consider your child's education?

A desire for academic excellence?

Recognition of a responsibility before God?

Complacency? "That's the way it's always been done."

Exhaustion?

Fear of failure?

A desire for your child to be a light in a dark place?

Socialization issues?

Health issues?

Safety issues?

What motivates us will color our perception of the choices we have. Each educational choice comes with its own framework. Each has significant structural differences with advantages and disadvantages.

As parents of children with chronic illnesses, we face an additional challenge. Do you have to take into consideration special busing issues, diet restrictions, special aids for the classroom, or consultations with the school nurse? Public school may have excellent resources for special education, but it can be tainted with so much worldliness that you spend the better part of each day debriefing your children. A private Christian or parochial school may have the values you're looking for, but does it have the capacity to deal with your child's chronic health needs? Homeschool offers a safe, nurturing environment, but caring for your child's health and academic needs may overwhelm you. It may make you feel as though you're sacrificing everything else to serve your child full time.

Whatever option you choose, protect your God-given authority by involving yourself in teaching your children; others must become *co-participants* with you in the process, not the directors. If you choose public school, know what the children are being taught. Think about ways to inject your Christian principles into what they are learning. Teach creation science through family devotions, for example, so children can debate evolution intelligently. Arm them with scriptural truth as a tool for making godly choices.

If your children attend Christian schools, hold them accountable for Scripture memory and challenge them to study Scripture on their own to avoid the trap of believing something "just because my teacher said it was so." If you homeschool, take them out into the community for service projects or hold group classes with other home-educated children from various backgrounds. Staying actively involved in the day-to-day academics, regardless of how or where your child is schooled, will fulfill your responsibility before God.

ELIZABETH

> *For the rest of the school year after Jordan was diagnosed, he*
> *continued in a private Christian school. He even started at the*
> *same school again the next year, but we had growing concerns*
> *about the size of his class, and he was falling behind in a few*
> *studies. Our main concern was his health. Any virus kept him*
> *out of school for a week, caused drastic changes in his insulin*
> *requirements, and meant frequent visits to the doctors. Then*
> *he felt overwhelmed and discouraged by the amount of make-*
> *up work.*
>
> *We were faced with a basic question: Which was more*
> *important—our child's health or his traditional education? To*
> *us there was no choice. We brought him home from school and*
> *had a fantastic second grade year educating him at home, and*
> *he had an incredibly healthy year. It was the right choice for us.*

We can't say what the right choice is for you. It will vary from family to family and from child to child within that family. The right choice might change from year to year as you are constantly reevaluating your child's needs.

The glimpses God's Word gives us of Christ's childhood are the scaffolding with which we build the framework of our own educational ideas. "The child grew and became strong; he was filled with wisdom, and the grace of God was upon him" (Luke 2:40). Think of each of these points as a strong girder supporting the weight of an area of development: As Jesus developed physically, he also developed spiritually, mentally, and socially.

DEVELOPING PHYSICALLY

As soon as our children are born, they begin to grow and develop physically. Physical strength comes from proper nutrition. Feeding your chronic kid (and your other children) a healthful diet rich in nutrients for their growing bodies will prepare them mentally for the tasks of learning. Your child's condition may require a special diet. Some children need high-fat, high-protein diets to encourage weight gain and growth. Other children's conditions require strict dietary limits on certain types of foods, such as wheat, food additives, or dairy products. And still other conditions may cause a child to be predisposed to obesity, in which case a low-fat diet is the best course. Ask your child's doctor to recommend the right book for your situation, or request a consultation with a nutritionist to help your family with your child's specific dietary needs.

Physical strength also comes from exercise. What form does your family enjoy? Bike riding, canoeing, hiking—even mall-walking is stimulating! Adapt exercise to your child's condition, but don't let that condition stymie the benefits of rigorous, enjoyable activity.

DEVELOPING MENTALLY

Children begin to learn at birth; they discover when they cry that they're picked up, changed if they're wet, or fed when they're hungry. Before long they become more sophisticated—learning to crawl and coo, explore and examine their world. We encourage them with toys, songs, conversation, challenges, questions, and instruction. Even children who are profoundly retarded or challenged in a physical way can and do learn. A person's intellect or lack thereof should not dictate our perception of whether he or she can "learn." Starting as we do from ground zero (birth), any progress away from that point is learning. Do children smile when smiled at? Do they laugh when tickled? Or, on a higher level, can they solve problems? Create? Interact with others on any level?

Education is a lifelong pursuit from the moment we open our eyes in infancy to when they are closed for the last time at the end of life. Our purpose as "parental educators" should be to instill a love for learning. How you reach that goal becomes the plan you use for your child's education. Do you like to read aloud to your children? Do you take nature walks and draw pictures of what you observe? The tools to forge a heart full of love for the gifts God has given us are found in languages, in the humanities, the sciences, or the precision of mathematics. God created us with a desire to pursue knowledge. All areas of knowledge originate with Him. "For by him all things were created: things in heaven and on earth, visible and invisible . . . all things were created by him and for him. He is before all things, and in him all things hold together" (Colossians 1:16-17). God is in all and through all and the basis for all.

We discover and learn constantly from God's delightful world. Everything that interacts with our senses touches, changes, and develops us in some way. God's physical world, our family, friends, literature, media—all impact our lives. We develop likes and dislikes. What we see, hear, smell, touch, and taste play a part in how we grow.

> *I had briefly stepped into the house to answer the phone, leaving my three small children having a picnic in the yard. When I came back out with the phone in hand, David (who has Down Syndrome) had unscrewed the cap from the oil tank inlet pipe and was busily stuffing strawberries into the pipe. After I calmed down and cleaned him up, I did a mental double take. His action, which had initially frustrated and angered me, actually showed me something about David's developing personality. He had figured out how to unscrew the cap (showing a strength in fine motor skills), looked for what would fit in the tube (using the powers of observation and estimation), found an object to try (testing a hypothesis), and then proceeded to prove his theory. He was thinking!*
>
> *Faith—mother of six-year-old David*

DEVELOPING SPIRITUALLY

Deuteronomy 6:4-9 says, "Hear, O Israel: The Lord is our God, the Lord is one. Love the Lord your God with all your heart and with all your soul and with all your strength. These commandments that I give you today are to be upon your hearts. Impress them on your children. Talk about them when you sit at home and when you walk along the road, when you lie down and when you get up. Tie them as symbols on your hands and bind them on your foreheads. Write them on the doorframes of your houses and on your gates." Let's look at these points a little closer.

Upon Their Hearts

"Oh, that their hearts would be inclined to fear me and keep all my commandments always, so that it might go well with them and their children forever!" (Deuteronomy 5:29). God's desire is for us to obey the laws He put in place for our good. God promises, "It will go well" for you and your family if you follow His commands. As the psalmist says, "The boundary lines have fallen for me in pleasant places; surely I have a delightful inheritance" (Psalm 16:6). God established those boundaries because He knew there would be anarchy and great unhappiness without them. Within God's boundaries lie the responsibilities we have for our children for their future. Caring for their needs goes way beyond the physical, even though their physical needs can take up so much of our time and emotional energy. We are responsible before God for the education of the *whole* child.

Impressing

Impressing God's standards and laws on our children's hearts requires discipline in our own lives. For them to have high expectations for themselves, our own standards must be high. Model behavior through your own daily walk with the Lord. Encourage them to put God's Word into their hearts. Hold onto the mental image of God's hand gently smoothing His words indelibly into your children's hearts and minds. His Word should be a seal or mark, sometimes produced under gentle pressure and yet fixed firmly into place.

In Favor with God

The goal of education is that each child would grow up to be a man or woman of God who will be about the Father's business. Developing character is the foundation on which all future learning is built.

Both of us are frequently asked to write references. When we get a call from a potential employer of a friend, the interviewer doesn't ask, "What grades did so and so get during her last year of high school?" Rather the person asks questions such as: "Is she conscientious in her work? Does he have a good attitude? Is she punctual? Is he reliable, honorable, truthful?" These are all questions of character.

We have already seen in a former chapter that having a chronic child often means that that child is put first. As parents we do die to self daily. That develops character in us as well as in our children. We learn how to stand up to conflict for the ultimate good of the child. Over and over we must grapple with our own weaknesses, forcing ourselves loose from our self-absorbed attitudes. We and our children grow "in favor with God" as our characters are forged through hardship.

. . . And Men

Academics are different from education. Academics are the means by which we educate, not the end result. The cataloging of data; acquiring knowledge; memorizing dates; improving penmanship; learning to read, write, and do arithmetic are all outgrowths of the purpose of education. These are all areas of "impressing" information on our children.

But to whom are you leaving the "impressing?" You and your spouse? Your pastor or youth leader? What about those who teach your children every day? What sort of character training will they accomplish?

Unfortunately, many Christian families unknowingly abdicate their God-given parental authority to public school teachers, guidance counselors, peers, and the media without realizing that thirty years of research has shown that no one has a greater influence on a child and his academic performance than that child's family—more than teachers, peers, or the media.[8]

MARY

We were in Wal-Mart having a photo portrait done of the children. There were several families ahead of us, so we waited patiently for our turn.

A woman behind me tapped me on the shoulder. "Excuse me. You don't let your children watch very much television, do you?"

I must have looked surprised at her odd question. She smiled. "I can tell. Your children are very well behaved." I glanced down

at my two hanging onto the edges of the shopping cart intently
watching the antics of an out-of-control boy who decidedly did
not want his picture taken. I grinned back at her and thanked
her for the compliment. I knew then that she was seeing the fruit
of six years of homeschool education.

People see behavior, and they judge acceptability by it. Why
didn't the woman ask Mary what her children's grades were in
school? She wasn't interested in how they were dressed or even how
clearly they could speak. She didn't comment on their physical
appearance at all. What she noticed was their character, which was
transparent. She had been "impressed" by a heart attitude!

It has been said that the greatness of a nation can be judged by
how it treats its poor, sickly, and downtrodden. Our culture focuses
on productivity, and often mental acuity is judged by such factors as
articulation and a drive for success. Society looks at people and asks:
Will they fit in? Will they impact this world in some way?

How does this attitude compare to what God values? Our value,
our faith, is in Christ alone. It is His counsel we should seek. All of
our actions, thoughts, and desires should be centered on Him. These
are the pins that hold the structure of education together. The pursuit of knowledge becomes the means of becoming more Christlike.

"It is for freedom that Christ has set us free. Stand firm, then, and
do not let yourselves be burdened again by a yoke of slavery"
(Galatians 5:1). Set your children free from the oppressive burden of
performance and concentrate instead on developing character.
Excellence will always follow.

PRACTICAL MATTERS

The dictionary defines philosophy as the study of the fundamental
truths of life and the universe. As Christians, we believe that all life
originates with God. To study His truths is to better define ourselves
in Christ. The same holds true when defining an educational philosophy. What fundamental truths do we believe in enough that they
should form the basis of what we will teach our children? If we truly
believe that God is the basis of all life, then He is the firm foundation

for our educational philosophy. The building of the structure becomes a matter of adding brick by brick to the rock-solid faith already established in our children's hearts. Without such a foundation, any attempts at building a framework will collapse like a house made of matchsticks built on sand.

Do you have educational goals for your children? Do you reevaluate them monthly, yearly? What do you do if your children are not meeting those goals?

Consider building an educational philosophy for your family, following this outline as a guide:

1) Enter into prayer with your spouse so you can begin your task with unity. Study appropriate Scriptures: Deuteronomy 5, 6; Proverbs 22:6; 1 Corinthians 11:3; Colossians 3. Note what God says about a parent's responsibility.

2) Write down all the defining educational values or "bricks" for your family (i.e., academic standards, godly role models, character training, etc.)

3) Group all the items into similar categories to develop the framework (i.e., scriptural living could go under the heading of biblical foundation, peer pressure under proper socialization, academic excellence under educational standards).

4) Streamline the categories to remove redundancy, combine ideas where possible, and tailor the structure to your personal situation.

5) Try to live within the framework of your philosophy for a month. If you find you've been unrealistic, revise your work.

13

My husband doesn't understand the consuming nature of my life with our children. The constant readjusting of medicines, preparing them for situations, and general organization it takes to keep them on target is exhausting. I don't work outside of our home because I feel that I'm already working full time, unpaid, and under-appreciated in my home. I need a break!

My dream would be to go away on a women's retreat where I would literally be cared for by others. No cooking, no cleanup, no orchestrating everybody else's lives. Just me, and God, and sisters in Christ.

Lois—mother of twelve-year-old Caitlyn with cystic fibrosis

TAKING CARE OF YOU

But those who hope in the Lord will renew their strength.
They will soar on wings like eagles; they will run and
not grow weary, they will walk and not be faint.

ISAIAH 40:31

There is nothing lonelier or more exhausting than caring for your chronic child on your own. We don't believe that the Lord intended you to bear the awesome weight or responsibility single-handedly or even with just your family. The task is too daunting, isolating, tiring, and confining. Have you recognized your own needs—time alone, time with friends, time away, a thorough break from responsibilities?

Caring for a chronic child (plus all the other tasks on your list) requires energy—physical, emotional, and spiritual. Your personal reserves need to be full in order to have the patience and wisdom to parent and care for your child. You can draw on these reserves for strength of every kind to raise your children.

FILLING YOUR STOREHOUSES

Your reserves are your storehouses where you gather up and store the resources you need to meet each day with a clear mind, a rested body, and a God-centered spirit. The need to fill the storehouses is a biblical principle evidenced over and over in personal relationships in both the New and Old Testaments.

After the angel appeared to Mary to tell her she was carrying Jesus, she immediately went to visit her cousin Elizabeth, who was six months pregnant at the time. Mary stayed with her cousin for three months, likely even witnessing the birth of John and staying for a short time after. Mary's pregnancy was perhaps as much as six months along by the time she left Elizabeth's home (Luke 1:36-58).

What can we learn from this example? These women were filling one another's storehouses. Mary stayed with aging Elizabeth, perhaps doing housework, caring for her cousin, and ministering to her. Elizabeth in turn shared her wisdom with Mary, perhaps teaching her how to care for children and be a godly wife. They both knew Mary was in an important position, and she needed tender care to strengthen her for the days ahead—not just for her trip to Nazareth, but for parenting God's very Son.

Likewise Job's three friends, who had heard of his troubles, decided to "meet together by agreement to go and sympathize with him and comfort him." Their hearts were deeply grieved when they saw Job's terrible condition, and they responded by sitting quietly with Job for seven days (Job 2:11-13). Words weren't necessary and might even have proved counterproductive. Just the presence of his friends ministered to Job. They were helping to fill his storehouses simply by staying at his side. (Though note: His friends later falsely accused Job of doing something wrong.)

Job reflected the God-given need in all of us to seek comfort in others and to turn to friends for reassurance. Later in the New Testament, Paul showed the same heart when he wrote, "Be patient, bearing with one another in love" (Ephesians 4:2).

As Jesus' mother discovered, sometimes God fills our storehouses to the brim before we even need the resources. It's His way of faithfully preparing us for a coming difficult time. It's only in hindsight that we see how we were prepared for the cup of crisis.

ELIZABETH

Peter and I had spent time alone together in Spain for ten days right before Jordan was diagnosed. Our trip was a time of personal and mutual replenishment. It was romantic and exhilarating. I came back having never before felt so alive; all my senses were on fire. Then five days later I found myself in the hospital with a critically ill child. It certainly felt like a bruising crash from the heights that I'd experienced in Spain. But regaining my equilibrium over the next several weeks, I saw that the Lord had been so faithful to give me that time of unity with my husband and a time of personal refreshment before Jordan got sick. I felt so grateful that my storehouses were full to begin with. I'm still drawing on portions of those memories nearly three years later.

Psalm 23:5 says, "My cup overflows." David was expressing how blessed he felt. There wasn't enough room inside of him to keep it all in. His storehouse was brimming over. But when parenting a chronic child, you may feel as if your cup is bone-dry and cracking from the heat! We know we need to have our cups "overflowing," but how, when there's not a drop of refreshment in sight?

The question really is what will fill *your* storehouses and renew your emotional reserves? How do *you* receive replenishing? Is it time by yourself, a quiet walk in the woods? Is it a meal with your spouse? Is it a girls' or men's night out? Is it taking a steaming bath and reading a book? Is it going fishing? Is it going to a movie by yourself? Is it a day window-shopping in the city? What works for you may be completely different from what works for others. The important thing is to think about what recreates energy in you. What will energize your body, spirit, and mind so that you are "overflowing," ready to minister to your family's needs again? What makes you feel alive?

GO AHEAD—TAKE THE TIME

It's so easy to fall into the trap of feeling guilty for taking personal time, but at the same time resentment can build as you are more and more depleted, and you find yourself lost in your child's identity and needs.

Caring for a chronic child primes you for the potential to become abusive toward him or her. Not to be offensive here, but the reality is that resentment and built-up anger can climb to a crescendo until the parent loses control. Frustration can eventually explode into verbal tirades or even physical violence. Rarely is violence against children a premeditated act. Rather it's usually in response to out-of-control feelings.

People often have a sense of loss of self when caring nonstop for a child with a chronic condition. As they lose their sense of identity, they also lose control. Such moments can do serious damage to a child—causing physical or psychological pain.

All parents lose their temper now and then. That's a normal part of being a parent. But striking a child in anger or yelling at a child out of your own frustration is unacceptable. It creates patterns of behavior that become generational. Your family needs help to recognize negative coping strategies and to learn new ways of coping that will edify the entire family.

Contacting your pastor or your local child and family services is the first crucial step in admitting that you are being abusive. They can direct you toward parenting classes, offer practical help, and refer you to trained counselors and organizations in your area.

One of the keys to halting abusive behavior is restoring your personal and spiritual strength. It's the full-storehouse principle again. The Lord wants you to have the stamina to parent your child with a spirit refreshed and filled with His strength. Even Jesus took time off by Himself to pray in order to regenerate and refill His personal storehouse so He could then minister to others. Note that He scheduled those times before and after He ministered. He had time alone with His disciples before feeding the 5,000, and afterward He went off completely alone (John 6:1-15). Other times He went off by Himself to pray or rest. His was hard work, and He recognized the need to wait upon His Father for the strength to complete the work God had called Him to do.

Does the Lord want any less for us? Does He want us so worn out that we can barely make it through our days? Jesus' answer is found in His own words: "Come to me, all you who are weary and burdened, and I will give you rest"(Matthew 11:28). Again, it's taking the route by which you feel refreshed and energized in order to find the rest He knows you need.

What holds you back from scheduling, accepting, or taking time for yourself? Is it finances, time, or child care? Do you feel you don't deserve it? That you haven't earned it? That perpetual exhaustion is your lot in life?

The Lord did not put you in this position of raising a chronic child to see you wither and die. His desire is that we always draw closer to Him to know His tenderness and to become more Christlike. We do that by setting aside time to fuel ourselves in His presence and by soaking in His Word. Is that something we need to feel guilty about? Certainly not. That's the way He created us. Hebrews 10:22 says, "Let us draw near to God with a sincere heart in full assurance of faith, having our hearts sprinkled to cleanse us from a guilty conscience."

There's always a way to get time for yourself. Mary finds that her work as charge nurse at a retirement home builds up her self-confidence; she knows she's a good nurse. Going to work is the break she needs and likes. A friend of ours walks at 5:00 A.M. every morning; it sets her day off right. Another couple we know, who work with a state agency, qualified for paid respite care for the children while the husband and wife took two days alone together. A creative family could hold a yard sale and with the money send the parents off together or, alternately, alone for a few days. Elizabeth spends one night a month at the house of a friend for a "girls' night" of talk and laughter.

A friend of ours talks about taking "mental health" days. When his life feels overwhelming, he schedules with his family to take a day of skiing alone in the winter or hiking in the summer. It restores his sense of self. Along those same lines, taking on a long-term commitment that has nothing to do with your child or his or her condition provides a way for you to keep your own identity. Joining a Bible study at a different church, taking continuing education classes on a topic of interest, or volunteering in a worthy organization—these are all ways of preserving your mental and physical well-being.

MARY

> *I've found that because I'm a creative person, my need to create and complete a project helps to replenish me. Even baking bread is a manageable, "completeable" project that gives me feelings of accomplishment. When Robbie has surgery, I usually bring counted cross-stitch with me to work on. It's a measured, tactile way for me to feel in control when my heart feels out of control.*

Another woman I know colors in a very detailed, precise color-
ing book while she waits through procedures for her child.

What will work for you? A renewed hobby? A class? Whatever it
is, schedule it, mark it on the calendar, and *do it*.

CO-LABORING WITH CHRIST

Jesus talks about the principle of "yoking" with Him in Matthew
11:29-30. He says, "Take my yoke upon you and learn from me, for
I am gentle." A young ox, not of full strength yet and new to the con-
finement of yoke work, is paired with an older, bigger, more experienced ox. The older ox helps to "train" the younger simply by steady
example. He acts as a role model of sorts and carries the heavier share
of the burden until the younger ox comes into his full strength.

Why did Jesus use this example for us? Because He is, of course,
the stronger role model for us as we grow and become accustomed
to our role of parenting our chronic child. The yoke we are bearing
is the burden of raising a child with a chronic condition. It's not a burden of despair or drudgery, but rather a recognition of the immense
responsibility the Lord has entrusted to us. We want to do the work
well; we want to plow our child's little furrows straight and true.

Sometimes relinquishing control to the Lord for your child is a
daily, hourly decision. And it is just that—a decision. You may not *feel*
that you are trusting Him, but at least saying aloud that you will *choose*
to trust Him pushes the door open for the feelings to follow. Think
about memorizing this or another verse of significance: "The Lord is
my strength and my shield; *my heart trusts in him*, and I am helped. My
heart leaps for joy and I will give thanks to him in song" (Psalm 28:7,
italics added). Repeating memorized Scripture over and over embeds
the words in your heart as a permanent, unshakable truth.

You need to feel secure in your co-labors with Christ for your
child's well-being before you can trust others to help you. If you're
stuck in insecurity and haven't yet reached a place of trusting the Lord
with your child, then you'll be hard pressed to trust your children to
another person.

CO-LABORING WITH OTHERS

Only you can be the judge of when you're ready to let others help you with your child. For some it may be necessary almost immediately after diagnosis to bring others on board as helpers. But other parents may struggle for years to find just the right people to help their family.

Empowering others to care for your child, beyond a break for yourself, has the added benefit of showing your child that his or her condition does not rule your household. Yet your child must feel "safe" with this person, confident of receiving good care.

Whom will you trust your child to? School teachers may have the most time with your child. Perhaps you can hold an annual training time with the teacher at the beginning of the school year, even inviting your child's doctor's office nurse to speak to him or her.

Caregivers in the form of baby-sitters, nannies, friends, or state-funded persons all need training for your child's specific condition. Even if they have worked with similar situations in the past, they need to be reminded that your child is unique with unique needs. Never assume that they are adequately trained or prepared to care for your child's needs. Invite them with you to doctor's appointments or give them literature to read. If it helps you feel confident in their understanding of your child's condition, you could even test them on their knowledge by watching them perform tasks or asking them questions. Try role-playing and practice crisis situations. You have every right to be absolutely sure your child is safe with the person you have temporarily given responsibility to. Always back up your verbal instructions with written instructions—it helps to eliminate miscommunication.

The right kind of caregiver for your family and child will depend on what you're looking for. Do you need just an occasional temporary caregiver? Could a friend or student fit the role with some training? Perhaps your lifestyle is such that your family needs a full-time helper who could live with you. Maybe a nanny/housekeeper is a solution you could consider (if you can offer room and board, they're not as expensive as you might think).

Any relationship you build to help you care for your child is dependent on clear communication. Every possible factor must be taken into account when you begin to co-labor with others for your child's care. Well-planned preparation prevents panic. Through note-taking, record-keeping, and written instructions, your child's teachers and caregivers can work alongside you to protect and care for your child, freeing you to pursue some private time.

ELIZABETH

> *We have had a college-age woman live with us between school semesters for the last couple of years. Even though she is only with us for a few months in the summer, it offers us a much-needed break. To choose the right person, we looked for teachability and the ability to follow precise directions. We arrange our brief times away from home around Jordan's schedule so that we set up the nanny and Jordan for a successful time apart from us. We leave detailed instructions, several scenario procedures, and emergency numbers. We also both carry beepers and cell phones with us. We're not embarrassed or hesitant to call home several times either, even if we're only gone for a few hours.*

Yes, it takes an immense amount of planning to leave home for a break, even just for an hour or two. But when you've planned well and know your child is in capable hands, then you can enjoy your break with the confidence that you are meeting your own needs and your child's. That's a double benefit!

WHEN YOU ARE ALONE

Single-parenting, either by choice, divorce, death of a spouse, or long absences of a spouse, is the most stressful way to raise a chronic child. You have no at-home back-up system. You are solely responsible for your child's care and well-being, and you carry that weight across your shoulders.

Our hope is that you recognize the essential nature of two key points to successfully single-parent your chronic child. Taking time for yourself couldn't be more crucial. Your child's health is going to be only as good as your mental well-being. Even an hour a week to yourself, doing something that meets a physical, emotional, or spiritual need (better yet, all three), may be just enough of a break.

Secondly, you need to have a friend, sitter, or family member who is trained in every aspect of your child's care to be "on call" for emergencies. We don't need to remind you of all the potential crises that could conflict with your ability to care for your child. Delays at work, car breakdowns, illness, and so on all need to be thought of and a contingency plan made for your child with a well-prepared sitter. Even go so far as to stock up on any medicines or foods you may need if you get sick and can't leave the house. Don't leave anything to chance: "An ounce of prevention is worth a pound of cure."

All this preplanning may seem fruitless if you never have to put it into practice, but if you don't have a plan, it's practically guaranteed you'll need one—soon! This isn't to say that the Lord isn't present or ready to intervene in your moments of need. His Word assures us that He is involved in every detail of our lives: "Even the very hairs of your head are all numbered" (Matthew 10:30). He is always available: "God is . . . an ever-present help in trouble" (Psalm 46:1). We look at being prepared, spiritually and practically, as double insurance: The Lord's supernatural help is always available, and our human helpers are equipped for assistance.

CREATING TIMES OF INTIMACY WITH YOUR SPOUSE

Personal closeness and physical intimacy quickly fall by the wayside when both partners are perpetually exhausted or overwhelmed. Yet the connection of intimacy is vital to your family unity and your personal well-being.

Men and women respond to crisis differently—we all know and have experienced that fact. Either person may shut down emotionally and/or physically for a number of reasons. Fatigue, a sense of not "deserving" pleasure, a sense of betrayal of their child, fear of pregnancy, lack of emotional or spiritual connection with one's mate—the list could go on. A woman in particular needs to feel an emotional connection with her husband before she can rejoice in a physical relationship with him. A man, on the other hand, frequently needs physical intimacy before he feels an emotional connection and closeness to his wife. Yet for both partners, sexual intimacy is a stress reliever, as "well-being" hormones are released. But how does a couple stretched to their limits with raising a chronic child meet these opposite needs?

First, it's important to recognize these are actual needs, not wants. Primary needs—physical, emotional, and spiritual—have to be met for a successful intimate relationship between husband and wife. When God created us as relational beings, He intended for all three of these to be met within a healthy marriage relationship. Each area must be nurtured, protected, and encouraged for both partners to feel "safe" in a trusting relationship. If needs in one area are not met, the other two areas will be affected. But how can you meet those needs when you're too exhausted by 9 p.m. to even brush your teeth, let alone communicate, pray together, and make love?

It's really a matter of recognizing that the health of your entire family rests on creating and following through on intimacy. The threefold closeness is the cement that holds you together through sleepless nights, worry during procedures and surgeries, new doctors, changed treatments, new helpers, and so on.

Everything worthwhile takes effort, a great deal of effort sometimes. A choice is required. To protect your sense of self, you actually need to be selfless in your marriage relationship. The more you give to the marriage, the closer you'll be drawn to your spouse. As your security in the safety of your marriage relationship grows, you'll gain an overall sense of well-being and "completeness." You will feel nurtured, protected, and taken care of.

How to create those moments or hours? If discussing intimacy is difficult for you, find alternative ways to "talk." Some couples leave notes on one another's pillows to discuss private topics. Other couples may light a candle by the bed to indicate they are feeling romantic.

Also utilize the caregivers we talked about earlier in this chapter and schedule a time to have an hour or two together away from home, even if it's just a cup of coffee at the diner down the street. Making the commitment to take the time and then following through sets in motion the mutual recognition of the need for time together. Once you follow this pattern for a few weeks or months, it becomes a habit, a guaranteed life-changing habit. For intimacy, be creative. Schedule to meet for lunch at home while the children are at school, or get a cheap hotel room for an afternoon if the children are home with a caregiver. On a Sunday morning send the children to Sunday school with a neighbor and stay home together for an hour. Let the children stay up late watching a movie and lock your bedroom door. When it's enough of a priority, you'll create a way for times of intimacy. Talk about what you both would like, how you want to implement a plan, and then set it in motion. You've got everything to gain for the preservation of yourself and your marriage.

Once again this is the co-laboring approach you're taking to build up your personal storehouses. You are co-laboring with your spouse through your marriage commitment, which ultimately removes some of the burden you may have been carrying alone. Where does this bring you? To a place of being refreshed and refilled, a place where the Lord Himself can shoulder your yoke to give you a much-needed break: "Cast your cares on the Lord and he will sustain you; he will never let the righteous fall" (Psalm 55:22).

PRACTICAL MATTERS

There are a number of practical steps you can consider for your child's safety and your peace of mind as you take a break and relinquish temporary care of your child to others.

Have all your legal and financial affairs in order, including an updated will and guardianship of your children.

Your child should wear a medical ID bracelet or necklace at all times, particularly when away from you.

Have a copy of your child's diagnosis, medications, and doctor's phone number in the glove box of each vehicle.

Train children how to dial 911 and how to communicate where they are, what the problem is, and so on.

Type out and laminate instructions for caregivers.

Type out and laminate emergency numbers, including 911, physicians, neighbors, phone company, electric company, and hang the list next to every phone.

Have every family member who is old enough and all caregivers take a CPR course. Call your local hospital or Red Cross chapter for locations, cost, and dates.

14

MARY

Early on it was easy to be overwhelmed by the particulars of Robbie's condition. In addition to his heart defect, he has learning disabilities. But as he's grown, so have I. As I peer down the road, Robbie's future doesn't seem so formidable. I am convinced of God's perfect plan for him.

I've found great hope and encouragement in Isaiah 40:10-11: "See, the Sovereign LORD comes with power. . . . He tends his flock like a shepherd: He gathers the lambs in his arms and carries them close to his heart; he gently leads those that have young." The sovereignty of God is displayed; He gathers up my child and me in His POWERFUL arms like little lambs. What an image! I wish I could draw it as clearly as I can see it in my head: Great rippling muscles, and yet His strength doesn't crush the tiny lamb. He cradles it gently, holding the woolly bundle tightly to His chest.

Lately I've been walking around saying "Hallelujah," another day to learn of God's love as this image stays etched in my mind.

EXPECTING JOY

In this you greatly rejoice, though now for a little while you may
have had to suffer grief in all kinds of trials. These have come
so that your faith—of greater worth than gold, which perishes
even though refined by fire—may be proved genuine and
may result in praise, glory and honor when Jesus Christ is revealed.
Though you have not seen him, you love him; and
even though you do not see him now, you believe in him and
are filled with an inexpressible and glorious joy, for you are
receiving the goal of your faith, the salvation of your souls.

1 PETER 1:6-8

"Be joyful always; pray continually; give thanks in all circumstances,
for this is God's will for you in Christ Jesus" (1 Thessalonians 5:16-
18). Have joy, pray, and give thanks. Notice the order of Paul's words.
Joy first. Why should we be joyful always? Because of our future hope
of heaven. "Faith and love that spring from the hope that is stored up
for you in heaven" (Colossians 1:5). Proverbs 10:28 confirms this
truth: "The prospect of the righteous is joy."

But can we find joy in the mundane things of every day? When
tomorrow threatens to be more of the same as today, our joy feels as
though it's dwindling to a thin drop. Times of discontent act as a
barometer to our emotions—cloudy with a 70 percent chance of pre-
cipitation. Our lives seem filled with gray clouds, tears, and foggy
uncertainty. Slogging through the day-to-day routine, we forget to
look to the shining hope of heaven. In heaven there will be no more
illness, disease, fear, pain, or worry.

We lose sight of our joy and future hope of heaven when we are surrounded by the daily temporal "ordinaries" such as: *Will Jordan's blood sugar be too high at noon?* or, *How well will Robbie do on his stress test?* Not that these questions about our children aren't important, but sometimes we get bogged down in the routine while the Lord's eternal perspective slips away. For now we are in the middle, caught between the glory and joy of Eden and the splendor and unbroken fellowship with the Lord in heaven. But Paul challenges us to remember the "unseen." "So we fix our eyes not on what is seen, but on what is unseen. For what is seen is temporary, but what is unseen is eternal" (2 Corinthians 4:18).

Our Lord created us as sensuous beings: Our five senses tell us all we need to know about our world around us. Yet we easily forget the whole of God's vast plan beyond what we can see, hear, touch, taste, and smell. We become trapped in our life patterns, for we've created blueprints to get us through each day. Our minds are boxed in by what we know, what we've experienced, and what we can't change.

But God's plan extends from before the beginning of time through the rest of eternity. As finite beings, we literally cannot fathom His timeless perspective. That's when we lose sight of His joy. Can we balance His eternal perspective with our temporal view?

SHIFTING FOCUS TO THE JOY OF THE LORD

We live in hilly New Hampshire. Most of our main roads meander over hills, through forests and fields, and follow alongside streams. We have no way of knowing what is hidden around the next bend in the road. A deer waiting to leap across the highway? A small washout from an overflowing stream? A three-car pile-up? Maybe a rainbow will be arched over a mist-shrouded field.

Our lives follow a winding path. It's impossible for us to visualize what God's plan is for us and our children down the road. Second-guessing doesn't change His directions. Preplanning doesn't mean that the bumps in the road are any less jarring. And meekly climbing into the vehicle and strapping in for the ride goes against every fiber of our being. We want to drive and be in CONTROL!

You've probably seen the bumper stickers that say, "God is my copilot." But if God is the copilot, who is in the captain's seat? God should not only be the captain of our lives but the navigator, the copilot, the gentle attendant, the very vehicle Himself. Switching from depending on our limited senses means shifting out of the controller's seat and letting God's eternal perspective direct us. There we'll find joy in letting Him take over. "You have made known to me the path of life; you fill me with joy in your presence" (Psalm 16:11).

We wrestle with God, who continually, patiently, and gently pries our fingers off the steering wheel and firmly points us back to the passenger side of the vehicle. "I know, O Lord, that a man's life is not his own; it is not for man to direct his steps" (Jeremiah 10:23). When we allow ourselves to be removed from the hot seat of control, we become the passengers. The view of the road is different, isn't it? And from that different perspective, watching the Lord as He deftly handles the curves and ups and downs, we can acknowledge our inability to guide our lives. In fact, if you turn from the temporal circumstances at hand and look into the Lord's face, you will see His love, compassion, faithfulness, and hope reflected there as He patiently navigates your journey. Often He will speak to our hearts saying, "Look at Me, look at Me."

God uses different means to gently remove the wheel of control from our grip. Sometimes His way is through crisis, such as an accident, injury, or illness. But the promise of His faithfulness in such situations is found in James: "Blessed is the man who perseveres under trial, because when he has stood the test, he will receive the crown of life that God has promised to those who love him" (James 1:12).

At other times we willingly relinquish control when we catch glimpses of heaven, as in a rainbow. When we see such a profound testimony of God's faithfulness (remember His promise to Noah is displayed through the rainbow), we can't help but know we're better off in His control.

Whatever method He has used to gently direct our paths, be assured He does it with love. As it says in 1 Peter 1:6-9, everything in our lives will eventually be used for His honor and glory. David wrote about static pain growing into vibrant joy in Psalm 29:11: "You turned my wailing into dancing; you removed my sackcloth and clothed me with joy, that my heart may sing to you and not be silent."

Our belief in Him must be absolute, for our hope is in *a living God*, not in a distant or elusive God, but in a living God intimately involved in our lives. When this foundational truth seeps through to the core of our souls, then the shift is made and the goal is near: Christ's complete control of our lives, which is exhibited in our joy.

ELIZABETH

I found it so difficult to feel joyful about anything for many months after Jordan was diagnosed. My child had a debilitating disease that daily threatened to cause serious complications and shorten his life span; how could I possibly find joy in that?

But I have found joy. When I've consciously looked for it, the Lord has been faithful to fulfill His promise to show me His presence, frequently through His creation. I've felt joy when as a family we have skimmed across a calm lake in our boat at sunset. I've felt joy when Jordan has awakened in the night, called to me, and whispered in a sleepy voice, "I just needed a Mommy hug." I've felt joy when we've calculated Jordan's insulin, food, and exercise correctly, and we've defeated the disease for another day. I've felt joy when I unexpectedly have time to myself, and I can take a nap, read, or pray. I've chosen to recognize those times as joy-producing, and then joy truly does spring from my heart.

God is so gracious! He knows beforehand what we each need to encourage us in our faith walk. "You hear, O Lord, the desire of the afflicted; you encourage them, and you listen to their cry" (Psalm 10:17). He knows what will trigger joy in our hearts. He also knows what will challenge us so that the heavy shackles of sin (self-pity, anger, fear, etc.) cannot break us but will shape us instead into Christlikeness. How do we know this? Because:

"God is completely sovereign.

"God is infinite in wisdom.

"God is perfect in love.

"God in His love always will *do* what is best for us. In His wisdom, He always *knows* what is best, and in His sovereignty He has the *power* to bring it about."[9]

JOY IN GOD'S FINGERPRINTS

Understanding God's perfect and divine love means we have no cause for worry or fear because "perfect love drives out fear" (1 John 4:18). God IS perfect love. In His perfection and omnipotence He does not forget who we are or what we need. "Can a mother forget the baby at her breast and have no compassion on the child she has borne? Though she may forget, *I will not forget you! See, I have engraved you on the palms of my hands*; your walls are ever before me" (Isaiah 49:15-16, italics added).

We are so precious to God that He carries each of us imprinted on His palms. What in your life can you see as imprinted by God? A moment of joy while watching your child achieve a goal or a split second in which God kept you free from harm? Do you see the rainbow as you come around a bend? Where can you look for God's imprints of joy?

MARY

> When Robbie was about five years old, we were headed to the hospital for yet another cardiac catheterization. My stomach had that familiar sick feeling I get every time we approach another of these invasive procedures.
>
> As Dana drove through the early morning darkness, I fell into a light sleep and dreamed I saw Robbie bending over trying to tie his shoe. As I watched, two enormous hands hovered over Robbie's bent body before tenderly scooping him up. Unaware that he was resting in the middle of the palm of these giant hands, he continued concentrating on knotting the laces of one shoe.
>
> I awoke with the image firmly in my mind. It stayed with me through the next couple of days. It was as if God was saying, "You see? Even when My child is performing the simple task of tying his shoe, I am there with him. I will never leave nor for-

sake him. He is Mine." The image reminded me of Matthew 10:29-31: "Are not two sparrows sold for a penny? Yet not one of them will fall to the ground apart from the will of your Father. And even the very hairs of your head are all numbered. So don't be afraid; you are worth more than many sparrows."

Knowing that our children always rest in God's hands brings peace. We begin to look for evidence of His presence. We can see the glass half full instead of half empty—and not just half full but brimming over with all the good things God longs to share with us.

Where in your child's life do you see God's fingerprints? An accurate diagnosis followed by quick treatment? A crackerjack nurse who worked to save your child's life? A new medication that has changed your child's quality of life? A wonderful roommate the last time you and your child stayed in the hospital? A neighbor who is ready in an instant to take your other kids during a crisis?

Even though you may face pain and disappointment because of your child's chronic condition, look for God's ever-present fingerprints and rejoice. Ecclesiastes assures us that "he has made everything beautiful in its time" (3:11). Can you imagine life without your child? Absolutely not. Why? Because you've felt the joy of the Lord in your little one's giggle or squeezing hug.

These are the Lord's faithful fingerprints, signs of His presence. And any fingerprint of God leaves its mark. Even unbelievers tend to see it. When we expect and experience joy, it becomes an infectious attitude, and people around us can't help but be influenced by it.

THE THREAD OF FAITH

MARY

During the same hospitalization when Robbie was five, I experienced what I call a "defining moment" in my faith. About a month beforehand, Dana and I had to decide whether or not to donate blood for the procedure. I was recovering from major abdominal surgery, and we had just moved. In order to donate blood we would have had to drive an hour and a half and spend approximately $100 to store the blood, without even a guaran-

tee it would be used. The prospect seemed daunting. So we prayed about it. We both had a clear sense from the Lord that He wanted us to trust Him and not spend the time and money to do this.

During the procedure a problem developed, and the surgeon had to do emergency vascular surgery to remove part of a balloon that had burst during the angioplasty. When we were informed of the ongoing complication, I felt numb inside. We had trusted God, and my greatest fears were coming true— Robbie would have to have a transfusion. But when we met with the surgeon afterwards, once he had assured us that Robbie was okay, my first question to him was, "Did you have to use any blood?"

He looked at me curiously and replied, "You know, I had a pack sitting right there ready to hang, but I couldn't bring myself to use it."

What a direct, personal answer to our prayers! Our joy was complete because the Lord had been faithful in answering this very specific prayer.

Scripture often talks about our walk of faith. This usually conjures up the image of a highway or at least a well-trodden path. But at times the road is hard to see, and it seems as if the way of God's holiness is not a highway, a road, or even a path. Instead it feels like a thin thread. Our balance is precarious, and we live fearfully, afraid our foot will slip. But remember who is at the other end of the thread helping us to keep our balance. When we are attached to God by a thread, a rope—whatever image you want to use—be assured *His grip* will not lessen.

George Macdonald, in his children's allegorical story *The Princess and the Goblin*, tells of Princess Irene who becomes lost on the Mountain of the Trolls. To find her way home, she must curl her finger around the magic thread spun by her fairy godmother. The thread leads her through dangerous caves, along a rushing underground stream, and behind the walls of the Troll Prince's domain. But as long as her finger remains fixed on the woven silver strand of floss, she is safe.

What a powerful image of Christ's love and protection! If we are connected to God by a *mere gossamer strand*, it is enough. If we feel a spark of hope in the power of God, it is enough. If we have faith as small as a mustard seed, it is enough. All we must have is that kernel of faith and hope. God's Spirit does the rest. That kernel, that spark, that infinitesimal strand is enough to guide us when it is connected to the God of the universe. And along the route lies joy, illuminated with a ray of hope, ready to encourage and inspire us to keep stepping forward in faith.

If God's love was great enough for our greatest need, our salvation, isn't it enough for the mundane needs, afflictions, and trials of life? Yes, it is—over, above, and beyond! God is into the details of our lives. He revels in small things, the particulars of your most mundane day. He longs to share every step of your journey with you. "For the Lamb at the center of the throne will be their shepherd; he will lead them to springs of living water. And God will wipe away every tear from their eyes" (Revelation 7:17).

He can and will "fill [your] heart with greater joy" (Psalm 4:7). Watch for Him in a rainbow, in a child's song, in a child's question. Wait for Him to reveal Himself through the miracles of life—the metamorphosis of a caterpillar to a butterfly, a puppy suckling from its mother, the burst of bulbs into the first bloom of early spring.

Inhale the fragrance of newly turned earth; smell His pure-washed scent of rain; saturate yourself with the heady perfume of roses, lilacs, and lily of the valley.

Listen for Him in the roll of thunder, the hush of rain, the laughter of your children. Hear Him speak as you read His Word—shout it out loud! Fill your house with ringing sounds of praise! "Shout with joy to God, all the earth!" (Psalm 66:1).

Taste of His goodness in a midnight kiss on the cheek of a sleeping child, a salty tear on a hurt finger offered for comforting, a succulent strawberry He created just for you to taste!

Joy is all around us. We need only open ourselves to it by having a heart of thanksgiving and senses alive enough to see, hear, taste, touch, and smell. We need only to be ready to receive every good and perfect gift from above.

Walk forward on your journey with God as your Guide, knowing His intangible presence is with you. This is the way of your life. This is God's way of holiness and wholeness. Are you ready for the journey?

> And a highway will be there;
> it will be called the Way of Holiness.
> The unclean will not journey on it;
> it will be for those who walk in that Way;
> wicked fools will not go about on it.
> No lion will be there,
> nor will any ferocious beast get up on it;
> they will not be found there.
> But only the redeemed will walk there,
> and the ransomed of the LORD will return.
> They will enter Zion with singing;
> everlasting joy will crown their heads.
> Gladness and joy will overtake them,
> and sorrow and sighing will flee away.
>
> Isaiah 35:8-10

PRACTICAL MATTERS

Use your senses to find joy in the Lord's creation around you. Go for a walk or simply stand outside for a few minutes. Use all your senses and feel the joy as you experience His creation. What do you hear? Beyond the drone of planes or vehicles, can you hear God's whispers of joy in the song of a bird or the wind? Step outside at night and be dazzled by the night sky. Read Psalm 19 aloud as a prayer of joy.

Suggested Reading

Stick a Geranium in Your Hat and Be Happy by Barbara Johnson
Bible Readings on Hope by Roger Palms

APPENDIX

GENERAL ORGANIZATIONS

American Academy of Child and Adolescent Psychiatry
3615 Wisconsin Avenue N.W.
Washington, DC 20016-3007
(800)333-7636
(202)966-7300
FAX: (202)966-2891
http://www.aacap.org

American Chronic Pain Association
P. O. Box 850
Rocklin, CA 95677
(916)632-0922
FAX: (916)632-3208
http://www.theacpa.org

Federation for Children with Special Needs
1135 Tremont Street, Suite 420
Boston, MA 02120
(617)236-7210
(800)331-0688
FAX: (617)572-2094
E-mail: fcsninfo@fcsn.org

Friends' Health Connection
P. O. Box 114
New Brunswick, NJ 08903
(800)48-FRIEND
E-mail: A48friend@aol.com
http://www.friendshealthconnection.org

Nathan News
National Challenged Homeschoolers Associated Network
P. O. Box 39
Porthill, ID 83853
(208)267-6246
FAX: (253)857-7764
E-mail: NATHANEWS@aol.com
http://www.foxinternet.net/web2/P. O.olerep

National Heart, Lung, and Blood Institute Information Center
P. O. Box 30105
Bethesda, MD 20824-0105
(800)575-WELL (Heart disease info line)
(301)251-1222
FAX: (301)251-1223
http://www.nhlbi.nih.gov

Pediatric Services
P. O. Box 60
Morro Bay, CA 93443
(805)772-6014
(805)771-9538
E-mail: info@pediatricservices.com
http://www.pediatricservices.com

WEB SITES

General Medical
AmericasDoctor, Inc.
http://www.americasdoctor.com

Dr. Koop, Inc.
http://www.drkoop.com

InteliHealth, Inc.
http://www.intelihealth.com

Medscape, Inc.
http://www.medscape.com

Mediconsult, Inc.
http://www.mediconsult.com

WebMD, Inc.
http://www.webmd.com

Educational
Council for Exceptional Children
http://www.cec.sped.org

disABILITY Information and Resources
http://www.eskimo.com/~jlubin/disabled

National Center for Learning Disabilities
http://www.ncld.org
National Information Center for Children and Youth with Disabilities
http://www.nichcy.org

OnLine Magazine

http://www.specialchild.com

For Kids

Joni Eareckson Tada/Joni and Friends Ministries
E-mail: jafphd@jafministries.com
http://www.familyhost.com/jetinaug/jaf/index.htm

SPECIFIC CONDITIONS

Arthritis

American Juvenile Arthritis Organization
1330 West Peachtree Street
Atlanta, GA 30309
(404)872-7100
FAX: (404)872-9559
E-mail: jaustin@arthritis.org
http://www.arthritis.org/ajao

Canadian Arthritis Network
600 University Avenue, Suite 600
Toronto, Ontario, Canada M5G 1X5
(416)586-4770
FAX: (416)586-8628
E-mail: CAN@arthritis.ca
http://www.arthritis.ca/can/

Asthma and Allergies

American Lung Association
432 Park Avenue South
New York, NY 10016
(800)586-4872
http://www.lungusa.org

Asthma and Allergies Foundation of America
1233 Twentieth Street N.W., Suite 402
Washington, DC 20036
(800)-7-ASTHMA (Information line)
(202)466-7643

FAX: (202)466-8940
http://www.aafa.org

Allergy and Asthma Network/Mothers of Asthmatics, Inc.
2751 Prosperity Avenue, Suite 150
Fairfax, VA 22031
(800)878-4403
(703)641-9595
FAX: (703)573-7794
http://www.aanma.org

Attention Deficit Disorder

AD-IN: Attention Deficit Information Network
475 Hillside Avenue
Needham, MA 02494
(781)455-9895
FAX: (781)444-5466
E-mail: adin@gis.net
http://www.addinfonetwork.org

National Attention Deficit Disorder Assn.
1788 Second Street, Suite 200
Highland Park, IL 60035
(847)432-ADDA
FAX: (847)432-5874
E-mail: mail@add.org
http://www.add.org

Autism

Autism Society of America
7910 Woodmont Avenue, Suite 300
Bethesda, MD 20814
(800)328-8476
(301)657-0881
FAX: (301)657-0869
http://www.autism-society.org

Center for Study of Autism
P. O. Box 4538
Salem, OR 97302
http://www.autism.org

National Autism Hotline/Autism Services Center
605 Ninth Street
Prichard Bldg, P. O. Box 507

Huntington, WV 25710-0507
(304)525-8014
FAX:(304)525-8026

Cerebral Palsy
United Cerebral Palsy Association
1660 L Street N.W., Suite 700
Washington, DC 20036-3121
(800)872-5827
(202)776-0406
FAX: (202)776-0414
TTY: (202)973-7197
E-mail: ucpnatl@ucp.org
http://www.ucp.org

Cystic Fibrosis
Cystic Fibrosis Foundation
6931 Arlington Road
Bethesda, MD 20814
(800)344-4823
(301)951-4422
FAX: (301)951-6378
http://www.cff.org

Diabetes
American Diabetes Association
1701 N. Beauregard Street
Alexandria, VA 22311
(800)342-2383
FAX: (703)549-6995
http://www.diabetes.org

Juvenile Diabetes Foundation
120 Wall Street, 19th Floor
New York, NY 10005
(800)223-1138 (JDF cure)
(800)533-2873
(212)785-9500
FAX: (212)785-9595
E-mail: info@jdfcure.org
http://www.jdf.com

National Diabetes Information Clearinghouse
One Information Way
Bethesda, MD 20892-3560

FAX: (301)496-2830
E-mail: ndic@info.niddk.nih.gov
http://www.niddk.nih.gov/health/diabetes/ndic.htm

Down Syndrome

Association for Children with Down Syndrome
4 Fern Place
Plainview, NY 11803
(516)933-4700
FAX: (516)933-9524

International Foundation for Genetic Research
500A Garden City Drive
Pittsburgh, PA 15146

National Down Syndrome Congress
7000 Peachtree-Dunwoody Road
Building #5, Suite 100
Atlanta, Georgia 30328-1662
(800)232-6372
(770)604-9500
FAX: (770)604-9898
E-mail: ndsccenter@aol.com
http://www.ndsccenter.org/

National Down Syndrome Society
666 Broadway, 8th Floor
New York, NY 10012-2317
(800)221-4602
(212)460-9330
FAX: (212)979-2873
E-mail: info@ndss.org
http://www.ndss.org/

Dwarfism

Billy Barty Foundation
929 W. Olive Avenue, Suite C
Burbank, CA 91506
(800)891-4022
(818)953-5410
FAX: (818)953-7129

Epilepsy

Epilepsy Foundation of America
4351 Garden City Drive

Landover, MD 20785-2267
(301)459-3700 (local calls)
(800)EFA-1000 (information and referral line)
FAX: (301)577-4941
E-mail: postmaster@efa.org
http://www.epilepsyfoundation.org

People with Epilepsy, Inc.
1313 Lexington
Plainview, TX 79072
(806)293-7378
http://www.o-c-s.com/epilepsy

Wake Forest University School of Medicine Epilepsy Information Service
Medical Center Boulevard
Winston-Salem, NC 27157-1078
(800)642-0500
(336)716-2011
FAX: (910)716-9489
E-mail: wfubmc.edu

Fetal Alcohol Syndrome
Family Empowerment Network:
Supporting Families Affected by FAS/FAE
610 Langdon Street, Room 517
Madison, WI 53703
(800)462-5254
(608)262-6590
FAX: (608)265-3352
E-mail: fen@mail.dcs.wisc.edu

National Organization on Fetal Alcohol Syndrome
216 G. Street N.E.
Washington, DC 20002
(202)785-4585
(800)66N-OFAS
FAX: (202)466-6456
E-mail: nofas@erols.com
http://www.nofas.org

Hearing Impairments
Alexander Graham Bell Association
for the Deaf and Hard of Hearing
3417 Volta Place N.W.
Washington, DC 20007-2778

(202)337-5220 (voice/TTY)
http://www.agbell.org

American Society for Deaf Children
P. O. Box 3355
Gettysburg, PA 17325
(800)942-2732 (voice/TTY)
FAX: (717)334-8808
E-mail: asdcl@aol.com
http://www.deafchildren.org

Deaf-Blind
DBLink: National Information Clearinghouse
on Children Who Are Deaf-Blind
345 N. Monmouth Avenue
Monmouth, OR 97361
(800)438-9376
TTY: (800)854-7013
FAX: (503)838-8150
E-mail: dblink@tr.wou.edu
http://www.tr.wou.edu/dblink/

Congenital Heart Defects
American Heart Association
7272 Greenville Avenue
Dallas, TX 75231
(800) AHA-USA1 (calls are routed to your local chapter
             or the Heart and Stroke Information Center)
http://www.amhrt.org
http://www.americanheart.org/Health/Lifestyle/Youth/index.html
(Youth section of the AHA website)

CHASER: Congenital Heart Anomalies—
Support, Education and Resources
2112 N. Wilkens Road
Swanton, OH 43558
(419)825-5575
FAX: (419)825-2880
E-mail: CHASER@compuserve.com
http://www.csun.edu/~hfmth006/chaser/

Congenital Heart Disease Information and Resources
1561 Clark Drive
Yardley, PA 19067
(215)493-3068
http://www.tchin.org

Kids with Heart
National Association for Children's Heart Disorders
1578 Careful Drive
Green Bay, WI 54304
(800)538-5390
(920)498-0058
http://www.excepc.com/~kdswhrt

Hemophilia

National Hemophilia Foundation
116 W. Thirty-second Street, 11th Floor
New York, NY 10001
(800)42-HANDI (Information Center)
(888)INFO-NHF (National Office)
FAX: (212)431-0906 (Information Center)
FAX: (212)966-9247 (National Office)
http://www.hemophilia.org

World Federation of Hemophilia
1425 Rene Levesque Boulevard West, Suite 1010
Montreal, Quebec, Canada H3G 1T7
(514)875-7944
FAX. (514)875-8916
E-mail: wfh@wfh.org
http://www.wfh.org

Hydrocephalus

National Hydrocephalus Foundation
Debbi Fields, President/Director
12413 Centralia
Lakewood, CA 90715-1623
(562)402-3523
FAX: (562)924-6666
Toll-free pager (Operator takes message) (888)260-1789
http://www.geocities.com/HotSprings/villa/2300

Inflammatory Bowel Disease

Crohn's and Colitis Foundation of America
386 Park Avenue South, 17th Floor
New York, NY 10016-8804
(800)932-2423
(212)685-3440
FAX: (212)779-4098
http://www.ccfa.org

United Ostomy Association, Inc.
19772 MacArthur Boulevard, Suite 200
Irvine, CA 92612-2405
(800)826-0826
(714)660-8624
FAX: (714)660-9292
http://www.uoa.org

Kidney Disorders

National Kidney Foundation
30E Thirty-third Street, 11th Floor
New York, NY 10016
(800)622-9010
(212)889-2210
(212)689-9261
http://www.kidney.org

Lupus

Lupus Foundation of America
1300 Piccard Drive, Suite 200
Rockville, MD 20850
(800)558-0121 (Information line)
(301)670-9292
FAX: (301)670-9486
http://www.lupus.org/
Also see listings under "Arthritis"

Mental Retardation

The ARC of the United States
1010 Wayne Avenue, Suite 650
Silver Spring, MD 20910
(301)565-3842
FAX: (301)565-5342
E-mail: info@thearc.org
http://www.thearc.org
Also see listings under "Down Syndrome"

Muscular Dystrophy

Muscular Dystrophy Association
3300 E. Sunrise Drive
Tucson, AZ 85718-3208
(800)572-1717
(520)529-2000
FAX: (520)529-5300

E-mail: 74431.2513@compuserve.com
http://www.mdausa.org

Neurofibromatosis
National Neurofibromatosis Foundation
95 Pine Street, 16th Floor
New York, NY 10005
(800)323-7938 (Voice/TTY)
(212)344-6633
FAX: (212)747-0004
E-mail: nnff@aol.com
http://www.nf.org

Speech and Language Disorders
The Unicorn Children's Foundation
7000 W. Palmetto Park Road, Suite 108
Boca Raton, FL 33433
(888)782-8321
http://www.eunicorn.com

Spina Bifida
Spina Bifida Association of America
4590 MacArthur Boulevard N.W., #250
Washington, DC 20007-4226
(800)621-3141
(202)644-3285
FAX: (202)644-3295
E-mail: spinabifida@aol.com
http://www.sbaa.org

Spina Bifida and Hydrocephalus
Association of Canada
167-167 Lombard Avenue
Winnipeg, Manitoba, Canada R3B 0T6
(800)565-9488
FAX: (204)925-3654
E-mail: spinab@mts.net
http://www.sbhac.ca

Sudden Infant Death Syndrome
Sudden Infant Death Syndrome Alliance
1314 Bedford Avenue, Suite 210
Baltimore, MD 21208
(800)221-7437

(410)653-8226
FAX: (410)653-8709
http://www.sidsalliance.org

National Sudden Infant Death Syndrome Resource Center
2070 Chain Bridge Road, Suite 450
Vienna, VA 22182
(703)821-8955
FAX: (703)821-2098
http://www.circsol.com

Visual Impairments
American Foundation for the Blind
11 Penn Plaza
New York, NY 10001
(800)232-5463
(212)502-7600
TTY: (212)502-7662
E-mail: afbinfo@afb.org
http://www.afb.org

National Association for Parents of the Visually Impaired
P. O. Box 317
Watertown, MA 02272-0317
(800)562-6265
(617)972-7441
FAX: (617)972-7444
E-mail: napvi@perkins.pvt.k12.ma.us
http://www.spedex.com/NAPVI

National Organization of Parents of Blind Children
1800 Johnson Street
Baltimore, MD 21230
(410)659-9314 (voice)
BSS: (612)494-1975
FAX: (410)685-5653
E-mail: epc@roudley.com
http://www.nfb.org

HELPFUL
SCRIPTURE VERSES

When You Are Afraid
Deuteronomy 31:6
Psalm 34:4
Psalm 118:6
Proverbs 3:24
Isaiah 12:2
Isaiah 41:10
John 10: 27-30
1 John 4:18

When You Are Worried
Psalm 119:169-173
Psalm 139:23
Isaiah 40:31
Micah 7:7
Matthew 6:25-34
Philippians 4:6
2 Timothy 1:7
1 Peter 5:7

When You Are Depressed or Discouraged
Job 11: 13-19
Psalm 34:18
Psalm 73:25
Isaiah 41:10,13
Isaiah 54:10
Matthew 14:27
2 Corinthians 1:3

When the Future Seems Uncertain
Exodus 15:11-13
Deuteronomy 11:18-21
Deuteronomy 31:6
Psalm 119:74
Psalm 126:4-6
Isaiah 30:18
Jeremiah 29:11
Romans 8:34-39
Hebrews 6:16-20

When You Question God
Numbers 23:19
Deuteronomy 7:6
Deuteronomy 26:18
Psalm 91

Isaiah 43:1-3
Isaiah 46:4
Jeremiah 18:1-5
John 14:18
Hebrews 6:18-19
James 1:17

When You Feel Contented and Thankful
Psalm 23:1-4
Psalm 90:14
Psalm 92:1-5
Psalm 95:1-7
Proverbs 19:23
Lamentations 3:21-26
Ephesians 2:1-10
Philippians 4:11
1 Timothy 6:6, 8
Revelation 7:11-17

When You Need Patience
Psalm 127:3-5
Proverbs 16: 21, 23
Isaiah 40:11
2 Corinthians 1:21-22
2 Corinthians 12:9
James 1:19
1 Peter 3:8
2 Peter 3:8

When You Want to Worship
Joshua 24:15
Psalm 19
Psalm 23
Psalm 29:2
Psalm 73:25
Psalm 100:2
Psalm 139:13-14
Isaiah 61:10-11
Colossians 1:16-19
Hebrews 12:28
1 Peter 1:8
Revelation 15:4

When You Feel Resentful
Job 42:1-5
Psalm 5:11-12

Psalm 131
Psalm 141:3
Psalm 145:8-9
Psalm 146:5-10
Psalm 147:3
Philippians 2:4
James 2:5
1 Peter 1:6-7

When You Need Peace
Psalm 16
Psalm 57:1-3
Isaiah 26:3
Jeremiah 29:11-13
Romans 4:20-21
Philippians 4:6-9

When You Need Hope
Psalm 31:22-24
Psalm 71:14-17
Psalm 130:5-7
Isaiah 42:1-9
Hosea 2:15

Zechariah 9:16
Romans 12:9-16
Romans 15:5-13
2 Corinthians 1:8-11
2 Corinthians 4:16-18
Revelation 21:1-4

When You Feel Love
Psalm 128:1-4
Psalm 133
John 15:12
Romans 12:9-10
1 Corinthians 8:3
1 Corinthians 13
2 Thessalonians 3:5
1 John 4:7-12
1 John 4:19—5:3

NOTES

Chapter Two

1. Charles R. Swindoll, *Intimacy with the Almighty* (Dallas, Texas: Word Publishing, 1996), 62.

Chapter Five

2. Joni Eareckson Tada, *Heaven: Your Real Home* (Grand Rapids, Mich.: Zondervan Publishing House, 1995), 45.

Chapter Six

3. Elizabeth M. Hoekstra, *Keeping Your Family Close When Frequent Travel Pulls You Apart* (Wheaton, Ill.: Crossway Books, 1998), 93ff.

Chapter Seven

4. Robert Perski, *Hope for the Families: New Directions for Parents of Persons with Retardation or Other Disabilities* (Nashville, Tenn.: Abingdon Press, 1973), 74.

Chapter Eleven

5. Robert Perski, *Hope for the Families: New Directions for Parents of Persons with Retardation or Other Disabilities* (Nashville, Tenn.: Abingdon Press, 1973), 51.

Chapter Twelve

6. Robert Perski, *Hope for the Families: New Directions for Parents of Persons with Retardation or Other Disabilities* (Nashville, Tenn.: Abingdon Press, 1973), 93.

7. Richard J. Fugate, *Successful Homeschooling* (Tempe, Ariz: Alpha Omega Publications, 1990), 5.

8. William Mattox, "The One-House Schoolroom: What Successful Families Do," *Practical Homeschooling,* May/June 1996, 54.

Chapter Fourteen

9. Jerry Bridges, *Trusting God: Even When Life Hurts* (Colorado Springs: Colo.: Navpress, 1988), 18.

The authors would love to hear from you. If this book has touched your life, or you're interested in communicating with the authors, please write to them at:

Direct Path Ministries
P. O. Box 103
Dublin, NH 03444

For more information about Elizabeth M. Hoekstra's books, view the Direct Path Ministries Website at:

Directpath.org